NEW DIRECTIONS FOR EVALUATION
A Publication of the American Evaluation Association

D1086373

Lois-ellin G. Datta, *Datta Analysis*
EDITOR-IN-CHIEF

Reasoning in Evaluation: Inferential Links and Leaps

Deborah M. Fournier
Boston University

EDITOR

Number 68, Winter 1995

JOSSEY-BASS PUBLISHERS
San Francisco

REASONING IN EVALUATION: INFERENTIAL LINKS AND LEAPS
Deborah M. Fournier (ed.)
New Directions for Evaluation, no. 68
Lois-ellin G. Datta, Editor-in-Chief

Microfilm copies of issues and articles are available in 16mm and 35mm,
as well as microfiche in 105mm, through University Microfilms Inc., 300
North Zeeb Road, Ann Arbor, Michigan 48106-1346.

LC 85-644749   ISSN 0164-7989   ISBN 0-7879-9948-2

NEW DIRECTIONS FOR EVALUATION is part of The Jossey-Bass Education
Series and is published quarterly by Jossey-Bass Inc., Publishers, 350
Sansome Street, San Francisco, California 94104-1342.

Subscriptions for 1995 cost $56.00 for individuals and $78.00 for institutions, agencies, and libraries.

EDITORIAL CORRESPONDENCE should be addressed to the Editor-in-Chief,
Lois-ellin G. Datta, P.O. Box 383768, Waikoloa, HI 96738.

Manufactured in the United States of America. Nearly all Jossey-Bass
books, jackets, and periodicals are printed on recycled paper that contains
at least 50 percent recycled waste, including 10 percent postconsumer
waste. Many of our materials are also printed with vegetable-based inks;
during the printing process, these inks emit fewer volatile organic com-
pounds (VOCs) than petroleum-based inks. VOCs contribute to the formation of smog.

EDITORIAL POLICY AND PROCEDURES

NEW DIRECTIONS FOR EVALUATION, a quarterly sourcebook, is an official publication of the American Evaluation Association. The journal publishes empirical, methodological, and theoretical works on all aspects of evaluation and related fields. Substantive areas may include any program, field, or issue with which evaluation is concerned, such as government performance, tax policy, energy, environment, mental health, education, job training, medicine, and public health. Also included are such topics as product evaluation, personnel evaluation, policy analysis, and technology assessment. In all cases, the focus on evaluation is more important than the substantive topics. We are particularly interested in encouraging a diversity of evaluation perspectives and experiences and in expanding the boundaries of our field beyond the evaluation of social programs.

The editors do not consider or publish unsolicited single manuscripts. Each issue of the journal is devoted to a single topic, with contributions solicited, organized, reviewed, and edited by a guest editor. Issues may take any of several forms, such as a series of related chapters, a debate, or a long article followed by brief critical commentaries. In all cases, the proposals must follow a specific format, which can be obtained from the editor-in-chief. These proposals are sent to members of the editorial board and to relevant substantive experts for peer review. The process may result in acceptance, a recommendation to revise and resubmit, or rejection. However, the editors are committed to working constructively with potential guest editors to help them develop acceptable proposals.

Lois-ellin G. Datta, Editor-in-Chief
P.O. Box 383768
Waikoloa, HI 96738

Jennifer C. Greene, Associate Editor
Department of Human Service Studies
Cornell University
Ithaca, NY 14853-4401

Gary Henry, Associate Editor
Public Administration and Urban Studies
Georgia State University
Atlanta, GA 30302-4039

CONTENTS

EDITOR'S NOTES

In day-to-day practice, evaluators collect and combine evidence to draw conclusions about some program, product, or person. Evaluators are in the business of reasoning their way toward legitimate conclusions that clients and other stakeholder groups can use. Reasoning is the basis for what evaluators do and what they tell their clients to do. But is the reasoning sound? Evaluative conclusions are often sources of controversy, and the inferences drawn from evidence always present potential loopholes for error. In what ways can the conclusions resulting from evaluations be trusted? How can evaluators reliably combine evidence from multiple sources into a final judgment about the merit or worth of something? How, and in what ways, can evaluative conclusions be justified in an objective way similar to empirical conclusions? This issue examines these kinds of perennial questions facing evaluators in every evaluation. Presenting several perspectives on reasoning in evaluation, the authors tackle some of the critical issues so as to stimulate analysis and encourage debate among evaluators.

Since its beginning over three decades ago, professionalized evaluation has spent much of its time and effort on developing methodological sophistication, and less so on logical sophistication. Understanding the reasoning process used to establish evaluative conclusions drawn in practice has to be the field's greatest unmet challenge. And the challenge is a significant one; to establish reasoning that leads to justifiable empirical claims in inquiry (that something is the case) is a complex task. The added normative feature of claims in evaluation (the worth of something) makes that task even more difficult, although not impossible.

By *reasoning* I mean a study of the systematic means for arriving at evaluative conclusions, the principles that support inferences drawn by evaluators. Primary interest is with what and how inferences are made and supported (the inferential processes) and with the quality, weighing, and marshaling of evidence in building a case (the evidentiary processes). Both these concerns suggest reasoning's goal of helping evaluators distinguish strong reasoning from weak or better from worse.

A discussion of reasoning could be an abstract and purely academic pursuit, but this discussion is interested in reasoning as it is encountered in everyday practice, as a practical matter. It is not a philosophical treatise on the nature of reasoning or formal logic, but it is a philosophically informed one. The treatment of reasoning is presented in light of relevant work in philosophy and informal logic.

In Chapter One, Nick Smith orients the reader in thinking about reasoning at a broad level. He argues that good evaluative reasoning depends on the broader social enterprise or "game" within which an evaluation is being conducted, because the game into which the evaluator will be entering when conducting an evaluation influences the development and justification of claims. The game defines the purpose of the inquiry, the kinds of the phenomena being examined, the outcomes sought, the procedural rules, and ethics.

Comparing two inquiry games, criminal justice and social science, Smith illustrates how the justification of conclusions varies even though the same evidence and phenomenon are under investigation. This case example shows the usefulness of the game metaphor in helping evaluators determine appropriate evaluative reasoning and the subsequent use of strategies.

In Chapter Two, I shift the discussion of evaluative reasoning to a more detailed level and offer the notions of a general and working logic to explain how evaluators reason to establish and legitimate claims made in evaluation. I contend that the general logic of evaluation overarches all the various approaches and models within evaluation. This specifies what it means to evaluate something, an activity logically distinct from, say, biomedical research. In Smith's terms, general logic specifies the game.

Subsumed under the general logic is a profusion of individual working logics. Working logic is the variation in detail in which the general logic is followed. It is specific to a particular approach in terms of the type of problem, phenomena, questions, and claims of interest to the evaluator. The concepts of general and working logic highlight some of the important aspects of reasoning that evaluators must consider in building strong evaluations.

In Chapter Three, Ernest House takes the general logic introduced in Chapter Two and focuses on one part of it, that of integrating all the data sources into a final judgment. This is a fundamental problem that faces all evaluators. House proposes a general approach to the difficulty in combining multiple facts, values, interests, needs, preferences, and measures into conclusions about the evaluand. He suggests that evaluators fit together all the available information into the most coherent account that results in an all-things-considered synthesis judgment. Critical to reaching the synthesis judgment is the notion of context because it constrains the options possible.

In Chapter Four, Michael Scriven summarizes some of the problems alluded to in part by the previous authors. He identifies eight reasoning problems that face evaluation today and examines two of these problems in more depth: the problem of how one can ever get from empirically supported premises to evaluative conclusions and the problem of when it is and is not possible to infer from evaluative conclusions about a program, for example, to a recommendation as to what should be done with the program. These are serious cracks and flaws in the very foundations of evaluation practice and theory. As Scriven suggests, a better understanding of fundamental issues and terminology and an explicated theory of evaluation are greatly needed.

The remaining three chapters offer commentary on the ideas presented in the first four chapters from three perspectives: informal logic, philosophy, and practice.

In Chapter Five, Anthony Blair provides a viewpoint from informal logic. Informal logic focuses on understanding nondeductive reasoning (in which the truth of the premises does not necessitate the truth of the conclusion). Much of evaluative reasoning is of this type. Informal logicians have proposed various strategies for examining the merits of nondeductive reasoning encountered in different types of practice. Blair highlights these approaches as fruitful avenues for use in strengthening and developing one's understanding of evaluative reasoning. He believes that the fields of informal logic and evaluation overlap considerably and can offer each other significant opportunity for the cross-fertilization of ideas that could lead to advancements in both fields. He encourages more professional dialogue between the two groups.

From the perspective of philosophy, Hugh Petrie, in Chapter Six, draws attention to what he sees as three common threads running across all four authors' positions on reasoning in evaluation: purpose, context, and synthesis. He points out that if these themes are fundamental to an understanding of reasoning in evaluation, then the authors share with the relativists a conception of purposive contextually bound behavior that permits relativism to flourish and undermines the possibility of reaching warranted evaluative conclusions. Petrie argues, however, that assuming the perspective of perceptual control theory of human behavior suggests to evaluators how to reach conclusions legitimately even though the judgments are inevitably dependent on purpose and context. Thus, to account for purpose and context without falling into a radical relativism, he addresses the threat by reexamining the traditional conception of human action.

In Chapter Seven, Debra Rog concludes the volume from the perspective of the practitioner. She argues that being continually self-aware of the reasoning process is critical to how evaluators make responsible judgments and weigh design trade-offs throughout the implementation of an evaluation. From her review of the first four chapters, she highlights six challenges for the practitioner and offers suggestions for keeping a handle on the reasoning process while confronting such challenges.

It is hoped that through these seven chapters, the reader will be able to think more clearly and critically about logical practice; to appreciate the central role of reasoning and its analysis in the successful practice of evaluation. The discussion illuminates ways in which reasoning is influenced and open to challenge and marks out the greatest hurdles. The many unanswered questions raised throughout the issue should serve as fertile ground in promoting further investigation and development into what it means to establish sound evaluative reasoning in day-to-day practice. One route to obtaining answers might be taking up Blair's suggestion for evaluation to start up an active dialogue with the field of informal logic.

Deborah M. Fournier
Editor

DEBORAH M. FOURNIER is associate professor in the Department of Diagnostic Sciences and director of educational research and evaluation, Boston University.

Understanding evaluative strategies as activities conducted in the service of specific societal games clarifies methodological issues and facilitates method choices.

The Influence of Societal Games on the Methodology of Evaluative Inquiry

Nick L. Smith

What is considered good evaluative evidence depends on the broader social enterprise within which a given evaluative inquiry is being conducted. Further, the question of whether one evaluative strategy is better than another can be addressed only with reference to the purpose of the broader enterprise in which they are both being used. In contrast to discussions of evaluation theory and method that focus on procedure (*who* evaluates, *what, when, where,* and *how*), I focus here on the purposes for conducting evaluations (the *why*). In terms of Scriven's (1967) classic distinctions, I will be discussing not the "goal" of evaluation (to assess worth) but the "role" an evaluation may serve (for example, to aid decision making or for accountability), although from a wider social perspective.

The context of an evaluation is a visible theme in this volume. Context influences the meaning of evaluative claims and the establishment of warrants (Fournier, this volume); and context constrains the possible interpretations and syntheses of divergent evaluative information (House, this volume). I am concerned here with how broad social contexts and enterprises shape the nature of evaluative inquiry, and I use the metaphor of societal games to illuminate some of these influences.

My thanks to Deborah Fournier, David Krathwohl, and Matthew Tynan for helpful comments on earlier drafts of this chapter.

Inquiry Across Societal Games: An Example

Any formal inquiry can be seen as an activity whose meaning derives in part from the preexisting social enterprise, here referred to as a particular societal game, which defines the purpose (the why) of the activity, the kinds of phenomena that are inquired about (the what), desired outcomes (what results), procedural rules (who does what, when, and how), and the dominant values of and sanctions for violating this social enterprise (ethics). Different games reflect variations within these parameters; that is, the purpose of inquiry in the journalism game (to inform the public) is different from the purpose in medicine (to improve health); inquiry procedures in astrology and astronomy differ, although some of the same phenomena (movement of the planets) are investigated; and so on. To understand fully the nature of a given form of inquiry, including how claims are constructed and justified, one must understand the various elements of the societal game within which it is being conducted.

The following is an example of how two societal games with different purposes and procedures give rise to different types of evaluative claims and claims justification. The example concerns two competing analyses by the Federal Bureau of Investigation (FBI) and the American Psychological Association (APA) of evidence related to the explosion on the Naval vessel *Iowa*. The example provides a balanced contrast of evaluative inquiry of the same event within the criminal justice game and the social science game, illustrating how the development and justification of claims may differ across societal games even when the same phenomena and evidence are under investigation. (See Poythress, Otto, Darkes, and Starr, 1993; Ault, Hazelwood, and Reboussin, 1994; Selkin, 1994; and Shneidman, 1994, for details on this example.)

In April 1989, 47 sailors on the USS *Iowa* were killed by an explosion that the Navy concluded was the intentional suicidal act of a gunner's mate. This conclusion was based on an "equivocal death analysis" conducted by the FBI for the Naval Investigative Service after an extensive investigation by the Navy failed to establish any accidental causes. The U.S. House of Representatives Armed Services Committee was critical of the Navy's conclusion of suicide and asked the APA to review the FBI report.

Although similar to criminal personality profiling and psychological autopsy procedures, equivocal death analysis (EDA) was little known within the psychological science community at the time. EDA is used by FBI behavioral science experts to construct a psychological analysis of a victim and to render a conclusion on the manner of death for cases in which police investigations have been inconclusive. The FBI agents do not collect original data but use evidence provided by the agency requesting assistance. For the APA analysis, 14 psychologists and psychiatrists independently reviewed much of the data analyzed by the FBI, and 10 of the reviewers concluded that the FBI analysis was invalid. All reviewers were critical of EDA procedures, methodology, and lack of a statement of limitations.

The event and the evidence were the same, yet FBI behavioral analysts and clinical/research psychologists reached very different conclusions—due in part to being participants in different societal games. Different purposes, social science versus criminal justice, gave rise to differences in what each considered to be appropriate types of claims and methods of justification.

The psychologists criticized the FBI agents for stating absolute rather than probabilistic claims, which would be more scientifically sound. "The conclusion is couched in categorical terms (indeterminate, accident, homicide, or suicide) . . . and is routinely offered with absolute rather than probabilistic certainty" (Poythress and others, 1993, p. 9). Poythress and others (1993) argued that many equivocal death cases may have to remain unsolved because unequivocal statements may not be scientifically warranted. FBI agents responded as follows:

> It is true that use of categories and the situational demands to choose a specific category offer their own problems. However, *homicide, suicide,* or *accidental death* (i.e., manner of death) are categories used by public health authorities in every jurisdiction of the United States. To make such categorizations is a principal function of medical examiners and coroners. Thus, it is the purpose of EDA, a forensic technique, to provide an opinion as to an appropriate category for a given death. We agree with Poythress and others that "the kinds of unequivocal, bottom-line statements offered by the FBI in its EDA report . . . are not defensible within the technical limitations of our science" (p. 12). However, they fail to note that although probabilistic statements are a function of some clinical and many scientific processes, the demands of law enforcement require that opinions be provided that do not equivocate. [Ault and others, 1994, p. 73]

The psychologists also apparently took all claims to be scientific claims and so subject to scientific ways of warranting claims. The FBI agents responded that although EDA involved some psychological aspects of behavioral analysis, it has never been promoted as a clinical-investigative method. "We consistently advised that EDA is not a 'clinical' but rather a professional opinion based on years of law enforcement experience with indirect assessment and violent death. This experience has, in fact, been recognized in courts of law as expert opinion" (Ault and others, 1994, p. 73). The psychologists agreed that the warrantability of such claims was a legal rather than a scientific issue: "the law of evidence determines whether mental health professionals may offer courtroom testimony about their conclusions based on psychological autopsies, EDA, or profiling" (Poythress and others, 1993, p. 13).

They also argued that "the EDA invites the investigator to go beyond the conventional realm of his or her presumed expertise (the person's mental state) and to reach opinions and conclusions about the legally relevant act itself" (Poythress and others, 1993, p. 11). The FBI agents countered that Poythress and others "apparently overlooked the fact that crime scene analysis and indirect assessment *are* within our expertise as investigators of violent crime, in contrast to 'mental health professionals' who are generally not criminal investigators. To offer an informed, expert opinion about the 'legally relevant act itself' (i.e., manner of death) to our 'clients' is part of our task. Our task is investigations and that includes the necessity of making judgments about what the offender did and why the offender did it. Our clients are law enforcement agencies seeking assistance in investigations within their jurisdiction" (Ault and others, 1994, p. 73).

The FBI saw EDA as an investigative procedure for arriving at claims based on expert opinion to assist law enforcement agencies. The psychologists (Poythress and others, 1993, p. 13) cited Rule 702 of the Federal Rules of Evidence (1990): "If scientific, technical, or other specialized knowledge will assist the trier of fact to understand the evidence or to determine a fact in issue, a witness qualified as an expert by knowledge, skill, experience, training, or education, may testify thereto in the form of an opinion or otherwise."

Seeming to emphasize the claims as scientific, they criticized EDA as a weak procedure due to limited information on reliability and validity. The FBI agents, seeming to emphasize the claims as specialized knowledge, countered that the claims were warranted on the basis of accumulated experience and skill.

> We agree with Poythress and others (1993) that reliability and validity evidence about criminal investigative analysis would be appropriate and desirable and could, in principle, be collected. However, the NCAVC (National Center for the Analysis of Violent Crime, the FBI division which conducts EDAs) has, for the past 18 years of its existence, devoted virtually all of its efforts to operational concerns, namely, assisting state, local, and other federal law enforcement agencies with the solution of violent crimes, primarily homicides and rapes. Our assistance has aided in the apprehension and conviction of suspects in numerous cases. Success is the reason our services continue to be requested by law enforcement agencies. Eighteen years of investigation into violent crime has enabled us to collect considerable case evidence about our effectiveness, and we have used this anecdotal evidence as feedback to improve the analytic process. [Ault and others, 1994, p. 73]

Emphasizing scientific criteria, the psychologists had argued that "simply citing customer satisfaction or gross evaluation of the general technique also fails to meet the requirements of reliability and validity" (Poythress and others, 1993, p. 12). They saw these justifications as similar to statements of subjective confidence made in areas such as eyewitness identification and clinical judgment. Similar statements in such areas often fail to correlate highly with objective evidence. In earlier testimony, FBI Agent Ault had commented on the "wonderful academic approach to a practical problem. It is typical of what we find when we see people who have not had the experience of investigating either crime scenes, victims, criminals and so forth in active, ongoing investigations" (Review of Navy Investigation, 1990, p. 253).

The psychologists called for legal restrictions on the use of such procedures as EDA on the grounds that ethical guidelines and professional standards were not likely to protect the public sufficiently. Reasons for this included "that professionals who use these techniques disregard the tenets and their colleagues fail to hold them accountable for this, and that some persons who use these techniques are not members of the relevant professional organizations and thus do not feel bound by the relevant professional and ethical principles. More troubling are employment settings in which professionals are not answerable either to governmental regulatory agencies (e.g., licensing boards) or to professional organizations" (Poythress and others, 1993, p. 13).

The FBI agents clarified their own position:

> We are law enforcement professionals who use EDA as an investigative technique when it is appropriate to do so and when, in our client's judgment, it will assist them in arriving at a conclusion. We are not "mental health professionals" and, when investigating cases, are not, therefore, subject to guidelines of the APA or other mental health or social science organizations. However, we are, and have been, answerable to our own legal counsel and the stringent process of scrutiny by the courts. The relevant professional and ethical principles are as real to us as they are to mental health professionals. But the standards binding us are dictated by the courts and the legal system, and the penalties for failing to follow them are severe. [Ault and others, 1994, p. 73]

The point of this example is not to argue whether the criminal justice or social science perspective is more appropriate, but to illustrate how the investigation of the explosion on the *Iowa* was being conducted within two separate societal games. Because the purposes, phenomena, and rules of these games differ, so does the way claims are made and justified. Is EDA as currently used a legitimate evaluative technique? Probably "no" within the social science game, possibly "yes" within the criminal justice game; the courts are still trying to decide the admissibility of psychological autopsies and related techniques such as EDA. Poythress and others (1993) cite numerous cases in which such procedures have been admitted as testimony and others where they have not been.

In summary, notice how the types of claims, warranting procedures, dominant values, and sanctions differ for evaluative inquiry in the two societal games.

Social Science. The social scientists believe that only probabilistic claims are usually warranted and accept the consequence that many cases may therefore go unresolved. They accept clinical judgments, but only when based on extensive experience and warranted by scientific evidence. Successful practice, as evidenced by client satisfaction, is not sufficient to justify a method unless correlated with scientific evidence, because a client may be satisfied with inferior results. They argue that accumulated case evidence does not substitute for scientific inquiry. They value objective, replicable knowledge and invoke both professional scientific and legal sanctions.

Criminal Justice. The criminal investigators work under a requirement for unequivocal claims, because some legal action must be taken. They accept expert opinion based on extensive experience and warranted by the courts. Successful practice, as evidenced by independent confirmation through apprehensions and convictions, is sufficient to justify a method. They argue that the scientific approach does not substitute for lack of practical experience. They value expert opinion of proven utility to clients and invoke both professional and severe legal sanctions.

Societal Games and Evaluation

There are many types of societal games, from the more formal games played by disciplines and areas of practice, such as science, religion, journalism, law, governance, business, education, and medicine, to the more diffuse, informal games of social movements and special interests, such as empowerment and social reform. The primary purpose of most of these games is not to produce knowledge or assess value but to solve problems, accumulate power, control resources, or influence the behavior of others. The activities of inquiry and evaluation are therefore instrumental means conducted in the service of other, higher-order ends.

Many social or recreational games are competitive: the goal of Monopoly is to put all the other players out of business. Similarly, many societal games are competitive, for example, business, and the resultant evaluation strategies serve that end—the comparative "best buy" techniques of product evaluation. Some social games are cooperative, such as building a sand castle. Similarly, societal games can be cooperative, as in volunteer charity work, with evaluative strategies better suited to that end—the participative techniques of community action evaluation. Social games can also be expressive, as in music performance. Similarly, societal games may be expressive, as in artistic production, with evaluative strategies suited to that end—the illuminative techniques of artistic evaluation. Inquiry and evaluative claims may therefore be instrumental, but not necessarily central, to the purposes of the societal games within which they participate. (Of course, the goal of some societal games often seems to be simple survival; that is, you just try to finish the game without losing all your marbles.)

The rules of social games are artifactual but nonetheless important to the performance of the game. Although societal games are more complex, rules similarly regulate how the game is to be played. In poker it is acceptable to misrepresent information; this is called bluffing. Apparently this is at times acceptable in politics, although never in science. One must "show your hand" when "called" in poker and science, although this is apparently not necessary in politics. In societal games, as in social games, there may be stated rules of how the game should be played and the actual rules of common practice (de jure versus de facto). In inquiry this is referred to as the difference between reconstructed logic and logic in use. The rules of a game may be considered fixed, as in the movement of chess pieces, or consensual, as in the rules for a given hand of poker, or in flux, as when children playing in the backyard change the rules as the game proceeds. As dramatically illustrated during religious reform and shifts in scientific paradigms, considerable turmoil results when rules that were thought to be fixed, or at least consensual, turn out to be in flux.

Societal games can also be characterized in terms of their dominant values. Because one cannot simultaneously maximize all values, each societal game has an implicit hierarchy of values. (For example, one is not permitted to shout "Fire!" in a theater because society places a higher value on public safety than on freedom of expression in such a circumstance.) In investigative journalism, the public's right to know takes precedent over the right of individual privacy, and the value of fairness is placed more highly than the value of objectivity (Guba, 1981). These values influence the nature of acceptable inquiry methods so that "both sides of the story" are sought rather than an "objective" report, and investigations into personal affairs are pursued just short of violating libel/slander laws. The dominant values of evaluation within a science-oriented game might be said to be the honest, dispassionate pursuit of knowledge about value. The themes of the 1993 and 1994 American Evaluation Association annual meetings, however, have been empowerment and social justice, respectively. These themes suggest a broader societal game of social reform, the dominant values of which might be said to be the compassionate pursuit of social redress. It is quite likely that the set of evaluative inquiry strategies matching these values is very different from the strategies most effective in the science-oriented game.

Evaluation Inquiry Strategies

In game theory, a *strategy* is a device for maximizing gain and minimizing loss. One could therefore view evaluative inquiry approaches not as models (Smith, 1994) or ideologies (Scriven, 1983) or even as persuasions (Stake, 1991) but as strategies used in the service of winning a given societal game. Evaluative inquiry strategies are, of course, only one kind of strategy that might be used to further a societal game; other kinds include planning strategies, communication strategies, organizational strategies, economic strategies, and political influence strategies. Strategies in which these other aspects dominate may be more effective in furthering the game (that is, provision of evaluative information may play a minor role in winning the game), suggesting why evaluation results may fail to have the dramatic impact that evaluators desire.

The purpose of any evaluative strategy, then, is to further a given societal game. How evaluative strategies do that is the topic Fournier (this volume) discusses under the four parameters (problem, phenomenon, question, and claim) of the working logics of the various forms of evaluation. The values of these parameters in a given instance (that is, a given working logic) are dependent on the goals of the societal game. The goals of the game influence what problems are addressed, which phenomena are studied, what questions are raised, and what type of claims are made. Central to all claims in evaluative inquiry is the evaluation of the evidence supporting those claims, and the probative value of that evidence ultimately depends on the degree to which it furthers the societal game that the evaluation serves.

A review of the evaluative strategies that have been proposed suggests that they do indeed serve a variety of societal games. To cite a few well-known examples, the methods of Rossi (Rossi and Freeman, 1993) contribute to the social science game, the methods of Eisner (1991) contribute to the educational criticism game, the methods of Fetterman (1994) contribute to the social empowerment game, and the methods of Brinkerhoff (1989) contribute to the business game. In evaluating a social program, which method is best? If the game is to promote social reform, then a strategy that mobilizes public opinion is likely to be more effective; if the game is to understand a social condition, then a strategy that investigates causal relationships is likely to be preferred. I suspect that many methodological arguments in evaluation do not concern which evaluative strategy is best in a given game but which game evaluators ought to be playing.

Although all evaluative strategies may have intellectual merit, and some may be more acceptable to certain groups, I am not arguing for methodological relativism. On the contrary, I am suggesting some of the contextual grounds on which methodological disputes can be resolved to determine best practice. The selection of appropriate methods must be made with reference to the societal game within which the evaluation is being conducted. Although social science may have been the initial game in which evaluation started, it is clearly no longer the only game in town.

For example, it has long been recognized that the methods that promote good science do not necessarily promote effective applied decision making. In 1890 Chamberlin, a geologist, argued that the techniques of multiple working hypotheses fostered effective scientific thinking but weak applied decisions. As a technique based on continual identification of alternative explanations, it provided a poor basis for practical action. That argument is echoed in the position of the FBI investigators who cannot wait for the certainty of scientific evidence in adjudicating criminal cases. House (this volume) takes a similar position in his argument for an all-things-considered synthesis judgment as a means of integrating multiple types of available evaluative information.

Conclusion

The use of the metaphor of societal games and the distinctions it suggests can be useful in clarifying issues of appropriate methodology in evaluation. The selection of effective evaluative strategies must be based on a consideration of which alternatives best promote the societal game being played. The Weiss-Patton debates of the late 1980s illustrate how considering societal games can clarify methodological confusion. In examining the disagreement between Weiss and Patton on the utility of various evaluation strategies, Chircop and I (Smith & Chircop, 1989) illustrated how Weiss's position reflected a policy formation game characterized by political rationality, whereas Patton's position reflected a program improvement game characterized by technical rationality. Using Habermas's concepts of purposive-rational action and communicative action, we suggested that these two games were predicated on different relationships between knowledge and action, which in turn gave rise to the effectiveness of different evaluative strategies.

Of course, similar evaluative strategies may be used across several societal games. Stanfield and I (Stanfield and Smith, 1984) studied ways to adopt inquiry strategies from the management consultant game for use in the improvement of the educational programs game. Indeed, a previous line of research on the use of other disciplines and fields of applied practice as metaphors for educational evaluation involved, in part, the identification of evaluative strategies that might effectively be transferred to educational evaluation from the original games for which they were developed (Smith, 1981a, 1981b). Some evaluative strategies, however, are likely to be acceptable only within certain games. The criminal justice system may continue to warrant unequivocal judgments based on expert opinion and may even accept scientific evidence as having higher probative value when it is available, but the social science community is unlikely to ever accept expert opinion over objective evidence. However, considering these issues within the framework of societal games does clarify the methodological and value trade-offs involved in such decisions.

Consider a final example. How might one evaluate the question of whether an incinerator is a good solution to a waste management problem? If the game is environmental management and one is concerned with the resultant level of air pollution, then mathematical modeling of incinerator impact on air quality might be an effective evaluative strategy. If, however, one is involved in a business/political game of control of resources and economic profit, then an economic analysis of financial issues would be appropriate. If the dominant issues concern quality of life within a social policy game, then qualitative case studies of prior installations or citizen surveys might be more appropriate. One would not use a citizen opinion survey to determine probable levels of air pollution, nor would one use a technicist argument to settle questions of quality of life. The strategy must match the game. This implies more than just that the method must fit the question, because both the method and question have meaning only within a specific societal game.

What is the best approach within a given game? Does measuring quality of life by a case study or a citizen survey lead to better social policy? Will mathematical modeling or studies of existing facilities lead to better environmental management of air pollution? These are fundamentally empirical questions whose answers depend on continued study of evaluation practice (Smith, 1993).

Understanding evaluative strategies as activities conducted in the service of specific societal games helps to clarify certain methodological issues and provides a stronger basis for making method selections. It leaves unaddressed, however, the very important question of whether there are some societal games in which professional evaluation should not play.

References

Ault, R. L., Jr., Hazelwood, R. R., and Reboussin, R. "Epistemological Status of Equivocal Death Analysis." *American Psychologist,* 1994, *49* (1), 72–73.

Brinkerhoff, R. O. (ed.). *Evaluating Training Programs in Business and Industry.* New Directions for Program Evaluation, no. 44. San Francisco: Jossey-Bass, 1989.

Chamberlin, T. C. "The Method of Multiple Working Hypotheses." *Science,* 1890. (Reprinted in *Science,* 1965, *148, 754*–759.)

Eisner, E. W. "Taking a Second Look: Educational Connoisseurship Revisited." In M. W. McLaughlin and D. C. Phillips (eds.), *Evaluation and Education: At Quarter Century.* NSSE 90th Yearbook, pt. II. Chicago: University of Chicago Press, 1991.

Federal Rules of Evidence, 28. *United States Code Annotated.* St. Paul, Minn.: West, 1990.

Fetterman, D. M. "Empowerment Evaluation." *Evaluation Practice,* 1994, *15* (1), 1–15.

Guba, E. G. "Investigative Journalism." In N. L. Smith (ed.), *New Techniques for Evaluation.* Newbury Park, Calif.: Sage, 1981.

Poythress, N., Otto, R. K., Darkes, J., and Starr, L. "APA's Expert Panel in the Congressional Review of the USS *Iowa* Incident." *American Psychologist,* 1993, *48* (1), 8–15.

Review of Navy Investigation of U.S.S. Iowa Explosion. Joint Hearings before the Investigations Subcommittee and the Defense Policy Panel of the Committee on Armed Services, House of Representatives, 101st Congress, 1st Session (HASC No. 101–41). Washington, D.C.: U.S. Government Printing Office, 1990.

Rossi, P. H., and Freeman, H. E. *Evaluation: A Systematic Approach.* (5th ed.) Newbury Park, Calif.: Sage, 1993.

Scriven, M. "The Methodology of Evaluation." In R. Tyler, R. Gagne, and M. Scriven (eds.), *Perspectives of Curriculum Evaluation.* AERA Monograph Series on Curriculum Evaluation, no. 1. Skokie, Ill.: Rand McNally, 1967.

Scriven, M. "Evaluation Ideologies." In G. F. Madaus, M. Scriven, and D. L. Stufflebeam (eds.), *Evaluation Models.* Boston: Kluwer-Nijhoff, 1983.

Selkin, J. "Psychological Autopsy: Scientific Psychohistory or Clinical Intuition?" *American Psychologist,* 1994, *49* (1), 74–75.

Shneidman, E. S. "The Psychological Autopsy." *American Psychologist,* 1994, *49* (1), 75–76.

Smith, N. L. (ed.). *Metaphors for Evaluation: Sources of New Methods.* Newbury Park, Calif.: Sage, 1981a.

Smith, N. L. (ed.). *New Techniques for Evaluation.* Newbury Park, Calif.: Sage, 1981b.

Smith, N. L. "Improving Evaluation Theory Through the Empirical Study of Evaluation Practice." *Evaluation Practice,* 1993, *14* (3), 237–242.

Smith, N. L. "Evaluation Models and Approaches." In T. Husen and T. N. Postlethwaite (eds.), *The International Encyclopedia of Education.* (2nd ed.) *4,* 2101–2109. Elmsford, N.Y.: Pergamon Press, 1994.

Smith, N. L., and Chircop, S. "The Weiss-Patton Debate: Illumination of the Fundamental Concerns." *Evaluation Practice,* 1989, *10* (1), 5–13.

Stake, R. E. "Retrospective on 'The Countenance of Educational Evaluation.'" In M. W. McLaughlin and D. C. Phillips (eds.), *Evaluation and Education: At Quarter Century.* NSSE 90th Yearbook, pt. II. Chicago: University of Chicago Press, 1991.

Stanfield, J., and Smith, N. L. "Management Consulting and Evaluation." *Evaluation and Program Planning,* 1984, *7* (1), 87–93.

NICK L. SMITH *is professor in the Instructional Design, Development and Evaluation Program, School of Education, Syracuse University.*

To justify evaluative conclusions, evaluators follow both a general and a working logic.

Establishing Evaluative Conclusions: A Distinction Between General and Working Logic

Deborah M. Fournier

We say we can evaluate almost anything. In our attempt to do so, we commonly begin an evaluation with a question to answer or problem to solve: what are the effects of the student at-risk program statewide? Is centralized adult health care better than decentralized? In answering such questions, we as evaluators collect evidence and draw inferences in such a way as to build a strong, plausible argument that is meaningful to an often diverse audience (House, 1980, 1992). Ultimately evaluators reason their way to a concluding statement or series of evaluative conclusions as to the merit or worth of a program, product, or person.

In making evaluative conclusions about something, anyone can then ask for reasons supporting such claims. Our evidence and reasoning, as well as our conclusions, are subject to challenge and criticism. The decision whether to seriously believe in and act on the conclusions depends in part on the reasoning used to build the case.

As with all inquiry, a fundamental concern is how to go about building a strong, credible case: what is the reasoning process by which evaluative conclusions are established and supported? In what ways are evaluative conclusions justified?

The means to developing, strengthening, and clarifying reasoning that leads to legitimate evaluative conclusions is the crux of successful evaluation theory and practice. Evaluators are in the business of establishing the defensibility of empirical and normative claims about some phenomenon to clients

My thanks to Nick L. Smith, David R. Krathwohl, and Emily Roberston for their insightful comments on the development of the ideas presented in this chapter.

and other stakeholder groups. The kind of reasoning used to justify conclusions is of constant concern to evaluators "largely because the worry about the warrant for conclusions drawn from *any* inquiry will not wane" (Phillips, 1992, p. 119). Furthermore, "the reasoning process behind evaluative claims is vital because at any one time, the viewpoint that is the most objective is the one that currently is the most *warranted* or rational. . . . If we give up this distinction, if we hold that a biased or personally loaded viewpoint is as good as a viewpoint supported by carefully gathered evidence, we are undermining the very point of human inquiry. . . . If a shoddy inquiry is to be trusted as much as a careful one, then it is pointless to inquire carefully" (p. 68).

In the attempt to clarify reasoning used to establish evaluative claims, I propose the notions of general logic and working logic. This distinction is introduced as a way to assist evaluators in thinking about the reasoning process that they go through in arriving at evaluative conclusions, to bring out some of the important aspects of reasoning that may yet go unrecognized in day-to-day practice.

General Logic

There are different kinds of inquiry across practice areas, such as that which is found in law, medicine, and science. Common to each kind of inquiry is a general pattern of reasoning or basic logic that guides and informs the practice (Toulmin, 1964, 1984; McCarthy, 1973, 1979; Redding, 1989; Taylor, 1961). This basic logic provides practitioners with the rules for constructing and testing claims, and it specifies the basic conditions under which rationally motivated argumentation can take place. That is, it specifies to practitioners how someone would reason to justify his or her claims. In doing so, it also serves to distinguish one field of inquiry from other kinds of inquiry. Without a basic logic circumscribing the inquiry process, there is only a loose set of activities.

Evaluation is one kind of inquiry, and it, too, has a basic logic or general pattern of reasoning. This has already been put forth in the logic of product evaluation advanced by Michael Scriven (1980, 1981, 1990, 1993). This general logic of evaluation is as follows:

1. *Establishing criteria of merit.* On what dimensions must the evaluand do well?
2. *Constructing standards.* How well should the evaluand perform?
3. *Measuring performance and comparing with standards.* How well did the evaluand perform?
4. *Synthesizing and integrating data into a judgment of merit or worth.* What is the merit or worth of the evaluand?

This general logic is also clearly evident in various philosophical discussions of value theory (see Hare, 1972; Rescher, 1969; Taylor, 1961). To evaluate anything means to assess the merit or worth of something against criteria and standards. The basic logic explicated by Scriven reflects what it means when we use the term *to evaluate*.

The general logic can be found across various instances of the evaluation inquiry process. For example, the numerous evaluation approaches developed by theorists vary from one another in many details, yet I find that they do share this common logic (Fournier, 1993). Connoisseurial, judicial, pluralistic, and goal-free approaches are all instances of evaluation practice (see Alkin and Ellett, 1990; Madaus, 1989; McLaughlin and Phillips, 1991). What counts as criteria or evidence and how evidence is weighed varies from one approach to another, yet all follow the pattern of evaluative reasoning noted in the four steps.

In turn, each evaluation approach belongs (or can belong) to a field of professionalized evaluation, namely, product evaluation, program evaluation, personnel evaluation, policy evaluation, proposal evaluation, and plan evaluation, to name a few (Scriven, 1991). Thus this general logic of evaluation is one that also overarches all fields within evaluation. It is the basic reasoning that specifies what it means to evaluate something, an activity logically distinct from, say, biomedical research. In other words, it specifies the game and the rules of the game that one is playing when conducting an evaluation in any field. If someone says that he or she is doing an evaluation, then he or she must be setting criteria and standards, measuring the evaluand along these lines, and synthesizing the information into a final judgment about the merit or worth of the evaluand. In turn, these four aspects of general logic are used to critique practice. For example, an evaluation would be objectionable if it determined that something had merit but could not provide criteria when required to do so. So the general logic helps distinguish evaluation from nonevaluation types of inquiry; it plays a critical role in defining and establishing professional identity and subsequent developments. (See Figure 2.1.)

Figure 2.1. Illustration of How General Logic Overarches All Fields and Approaches Within Evaluation

General Logic of Evaluation

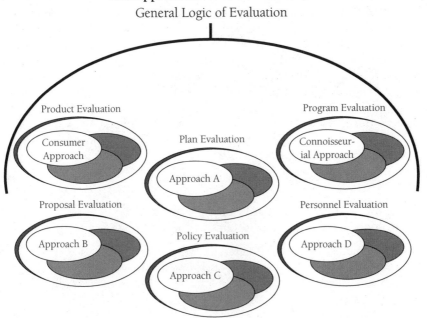

The evaluation inquiry game, to use Smith's term (see Chapter One), comes from an evaluative point of view in making evaluative types of claims by following the rules of this general logic in answering the following question: what is it to rationally assert the merit or worth of X? Although the various approaches found within the different fields follow this logic, they answer this question differently.

Working Logic

Subsumed under the general logic are many individual working logics. Working logic is the variation in detail in which the general logic is followed when conducting an evaluation. In other words, what varies across approaches is what or how criteria are identified, what or how standards are constructed, how performance is measured, and how data are synthesized. For example, in a consumer approach to product evaluation a source of criteria is the properties inherent in the product (Scriven, 1980, 1981). In contrast, others have suggested that a source of criteria for evaluating social programs is what stakeholders value in a particular program (Shadish, Cook, and Leviton, 1991) or values personally held by an expert (Eisner, 1989, 1991).

Working logic is a term taken from the work of Stephen Toulmin (1964, 1972) and is tied to his characterization of disciplines as rational enterprises. Using Abraham Kaplan's (1964) distinction between reconstructed logic and logic-in-use, working logic is the logic-in-use found in everyday practice to establish and justify evaluative claims.

Each evaluation approach has its own working logic. Working logic guides and informs evaluators about how to reason to justify conclusions using a specific evaluation approach. By analogy, general logic is the strategy and working logic is the specific tactic. To justify conclusions made in evaluation, evaluators follow both forms of logic. Evaluators all follow the same general logic and employ a particular instance of it, a working logic. And theorists advance both kinds of logic in the approaches to practice they advocate.

There are two different ways of thinking about working logic in evaluation. First, working logic can be conceptualized as a set of four parameters that circumscribe the boundaries in which the reasoning process takes place: problem, phenomenon, question, and claim. Second, working logic can be conceptualized as an argument structure that reveals the reasoning pattern used to support conclusions.

Working Logic as Four Parameters: Problem, Phenomenon, Question, and Claim

Across evaluations there are differences in how the four steps of the general logic are followed. In step 1, the set of criteria identified can vary from evaluation to evaluation depending on the kind of evaluand under study. To identify criteria against which the evaluand will be measured in a particular study, a clear understanding of the phenomenon is first needed (Scriven, 1980, 1981). This does not simply mean that an evaluator must know what he or she is evaluating but rather that he or she have a thorough understanding of its parts, organization, or structure; how it works; and how it relates to the larger context. Without this deep-seated feel for the phenomenon, the evaluator may select inappropriate criteria and omit critical ones. This is a serious problem; criteria can make or break an evaluation because they establish the basis for evaluative conclusions and thus directly affect the validity of claims.

Criteria selection is also influenced by the kind of questions being asked in the inquiry. A clear formulation of the questions is needed to identify meaningful criteria. Understanding what kind of phenomenon is involved in a certain evaluation and what kind of question is being asked influences step 1 of the general logic. This, of course, influences the standards that are constructed in step 2. In turn, the kind of questions posed will obviously influence the kind of conclusions or claims drawn in step 4.

The kind of phenomena, questions, and claims are shaped by the kind of problem addressed in a particular evaluation. Also, in measuring the evaluand, the kind of problem being investigated influences how measures are to be taken (step 3). For instance, in a connoisseurial approach the problem is to describe the unique qualities of a program. Expert observation of participants is an appropriate means for this. However, such direct observation may be inappropriate for getting at causal relationships when dealing with problems of intervention effectiveness.

Thus differences in how the general logic is followed are due to the particular type of problems addressed by an evaluation, which in turn influences how the phenomenon under study is (or can be) defined, the kinds of questions raised about the phenomenon, and the kinds of claims that are ultimately made in the inquiry. These are the four parameters that circumscribe the boundaries of a given working logic: problem, phenomenon, question, and claim. (See Figure 2.2. Note that the parameters and steps are obviously interwoven and thus do not fit neatly in any one place. For the sake of categorizing the variation within general logic, the figure loses the sense of interaction among parameters.)

These parameters of working logic set the foundation for building an argument that works to establish and support conclusions (that is, reasoning is directed toward this particular set of parameters). Each evaluation approach has its own set of values for these parameters. Every theorist advances not only a particular approach but also a particular set of parameters—a certain way to establish evaluative conclusions. And because evaluation practice varies widely along these four parameters, evaluation practice can be viewed as consisting of a profusion of individual working logics.

For example, the working logic of a consumer approach to product evaluation (Scriven, 1981, 1990, 1993) focuses on determining the extent of performance (the problem) of functional products such as computers or cars (the phenomenon). The goal is to establish a performance/value conclusion (the

Figure 2.2. The Relationship Between Working Logic and General Logic

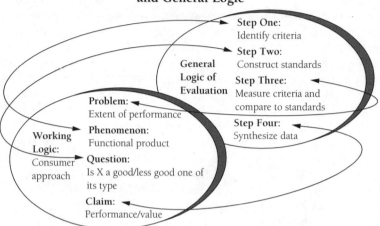

claim) that answers questions such as Is *X* a good one of its type? Is this *X* good or less good when compared with other *X*'s? (the question).

In contrast, a connoisseurial approach to program evaluation (Eisner, 1989, 1991) focuses on describing the unique qualities of a program (the problem) that is defined as a collection of qualities (the phenomenon). Its goal is to establish a descriptive or value conclusion (the claim) that answers questions such as What does it feel like to be in this program (as perceived by this expert)? What are the qualities that make this program good or less than good?

Still, a causal approach to program evaluation focuses on determining the intervention effectiveness of a program (the problem) that is defined as a set of treatment-outcome relationships (the phenomenon). The relationship has been structured in such a way as to ameliorate a particular educational or social problem. The goal is to a establish a causal or value conclusion (the claim) that answers questions such as Is *A* more effective than *B* in producing *X*? Does program *A* cause more of *X* than program *B*? (the question) (Cook, 1991; Cook and Campbell, 1979). This approach obviously differs along all four parameters of working logic when compared with a consumer approach to product evaluation or a connoisseurial approach to program evaluation. (See Figures 2.3 and 2.4.)

Notice in these examples that the connoisseurial and causal approaches both deal with programs. Although on one level both approaches deal with the same type of phenomenon, namely programs, the phenomenon is different in that the approaches differ in the way programs are defined or conceptualized; that is, each has a different social construction. A causal approach defines a program as a set of treatment-outcome relationships. A connoisseurial approach defines a program as a collection of unique qualities. The two approaches therefore deal with different phenomena (and ask different questions of them). These approaches use two different kinds of working logic within the field of program evaluation.

Figure 2.3. Parameters of Different Working Logics

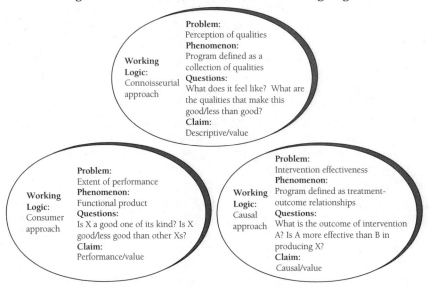

Figure 2.4. Individual Working Logics Subsumed Under the General Logic

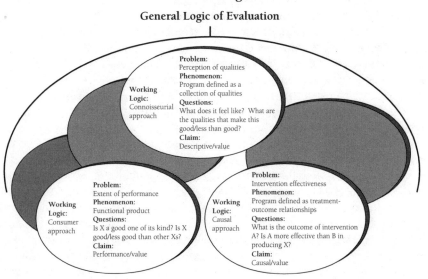

Typically, evaluation approaches (that is, working logics) are developed in one field of evaluation. But it may be fruitful to employ an approach in other fields. For example, a causal approach to program evaluation might be used in product evaluation. A product could be defined as a set of treatment-outcome relationships, questions concerning cause and effect could be asked about products (such as prescription and nonprescription drugs or durable medical equipment such as wheelchairs, walkers, and the like). Yet it might not make sense to use the same approach in, say, policy evaluation. Or a consumer approach to product evaluation might be used in program evaluation. A program could be defined as a functional product; that is, program goals could be viewed as the functional properties of a program. In fact, we are all familiar with the long-standing objectives-based or goal-based approaches to evaluation that focus solely on evaluating the extent to which program objectives or goals have been attained. So parameters can be examined for their applicability in various fields. They are the ways in which we would expect approaches to differ.

One last point is that how the phenomenon is defined (that is, socially constructed) is important because it influences the source or locus of values from which criteria are selected (step 1 of the general logic). In turn, criteria selection affects the validity of conclusions because it influences the reasoning used in establishing them. The reasoning is affected because the source of the criteria commits us to look for certain kinds of evidence and to appeal to certain kinds of warrants in order to justify resulting claims. In other words, how evaluators reason toward evaluative judgments depends on how value (criteria) is defined. Thus, the burden of justification rests on the criteria.[1]

For example, in a connoisseurial approach to program evaluation the goal is to reveal the qualities of the program as perceived by an expert so that others can see and feel what it is like to be in that program, the program being defined here as a set of qualities (Eisner 1989, 1991). The approach reasons toward a judgment of merit or worth concerning some of the qualities of a program. Given that the source of criteria is personally held values of an expert, then the kind of evidence an evaluator would be expected to look for would be a statement of these values. To infer that a program is good according to this expert is to then expect an evaluator to appeal to warrants that assert that this expert's judgment is reliable. To warrant claims in this approach is to affirm the credibility and reliability of the expert.

In contrast, in a pluralistic approach to program evaluation, the phenomenon of interest is, again, a program, but it is defined as a set of values and expectations that are held for a program by its stakeholders (Shadish, Cook, and Leviton, 1991; Stake, 1989, 1991). The approach reasons toward a description of a program so that decision makers and other stakeholders can vicariously experience what it is like to be involved in that program. In this approach it is primarily stakeholder values that are required to evaluate the merits of a program. Given that the source of criteria is stakeholder values, then the kind of evidence an evaluator would be expected to look for would be a statement of these values. To infer program impact based on the evidence of values is to expect an evaluator to appeal to warrants that assert that stakeholder values is motive enough for accepting the conclusion because the program aims to serve stakeholders, and they are in the best position to know what that service should be like. (See Table 2.1 for additional examples.)

Therefore the first step of the general logic and the parameter of phenomenon is the most crucial concern for evaluators. Seeing theorists as developing alternative working logics for evaluation practice, thus committing them to take somewhat different stances toward the making and justifying of evaluative claims, suggests that perhaps the various debates about what constitutes good evaluations are often really hidden differences about how the phenomenon is viewed.

Working Logic as a Reasoning Pattern

A second way to conceptualize working logic is as an argument structure that makes concrete the reasoning pattern by which conclusions are justified. Whereas the parameters define the scope of a particular working logic, this

Table 2.1. Comparison of Different Definitions for the Same Phenomenon

Evaluation Approach	Phenomenon of Interest	Source of Criteria (Locus of Values)	Evidence (Foundation for a Claim)	Warrant (authorizes Inference)
Connoisseurial/ critic approach to program evaluation	Program defined as set of qualities identifiable by an expert	Personally held values of an expert	Expert values	Expert is reliable and credible
Pluralistic approach to program evaluation	Program defined as set of values held by stakeholders	Stakeholder values	Stakeholder values and their connection to impact	Stakeholder values reflect what is desirable and important
Consumer approach to product evaluation	Functional product	Properties inherent in the product and consumer use	Properties and their connection to extent of performance	Accepted meaning of the word (such as car or watch)
Goal-free approach to program evaluation	Program defined as a means of meeting needs	Consumer needs	Needs and their connection to program effects	Needs accepted as necessary requirements for existence
Causal approach to program evaluation	Program defined as set of treatment-outcome relationships	Dependent variables in goals or research literature	Relationships among variables	Relationships were identified under reliable methods

second conceptualization lays out the reasoning pattern used to justify conclusions within given parameters.

Stephen Toulmin (1964) examined different types of inquiry and found that inquiry is best characterized as the building of a defensible argument. He identified six logical features that are common to all kinds of inquiry. All these features work together to support and justify conclusions resulting from a process of inquiry:

Claims that conclude what is to be taken as acceptable and legitimate
Evidence, that is, the facts forming the basis for the claim
Warrants that legitimate the inferences drawn from evidence by appeal to some authority
Backings that support the warrant by appeal to some more general authority
Conditions of exception that point out circumstances when the warrant may not hold
Qualifiers that identify the strength of the claim (see Figure 2.5).

This argument structure can be a useful tool in mapping out the reasoning process in any evaluation. In earlier work, I have explained each feature in detail and applied it to some of the evaluation approaches in order to clarify

Figure 2.5. Six Main Logical Features Common to All Inquiry

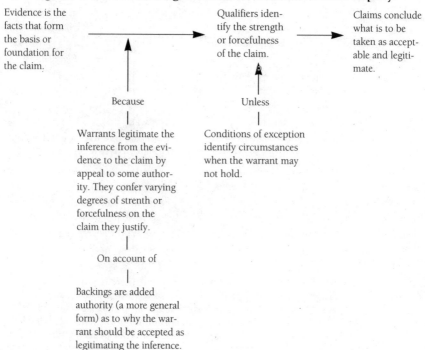

Evidence is the facts that form the basis or foundation for the claim.

Qualifiers identify the strength or forcefulness of the claim.

Claims conclude what is to be taken as acceptable and legitimate.

Because

Unless

Warrants legitimate the inference from the evidence to the claim by appeal to some authority. They confer varying degrees of strenth or forcefulness on the claim they justify.

Conditions of exception identify circumstances when the warrant may not hold.

On account of

Backings are added authority (a more general form) as to why the warrant should be accepted as legitimating the inference.

the merit of each approach. (See Fournier 1992; Fournier and Smith, 1993.) In this work I applied the features and used them to explicate and summarize the overall reasoning of a particular evaluation approach. But typically an overall argument contains a collection of subarguments linked together in various configurations. The structure is useful in mapping underlying subarguments because more than single pieces of evidence, warrants, backings, conditions of exception, and qualifiers are usually offered to support and legitimate claims made in evaluations. The structure is a useful concept to examine reasoning at multiple levels.

In the previous section I stated that parameters of working logic can vary across evaluation approaches. Although one parameter, the type of claim, may vary across different working logics, all claims are similar in that they depend on five logical features of an argument: evidence, warrant, backing, conditions of exception, and qualifier. Given space constraints, I will discuss only one of these features in this chapter, the warrant, to suggest one way in which this tool can be useful.

Warrant-Establishing Versus Warrant-Using

The warrant is what legitimates the inferences drawn from evidence by appeal to some kind of authority. The warrants on which claims rely vary from one area of practice to another. Certain kinds of warrant are deemed acceptable by members within an area of practice. For instance, in science claims are made about causation by appeal to the randomization of samples. Appeals to another authority such as "because I saw it with my own eyes" or "because God revealed it to me" would not be acceptable warrants for causal claims, although such appeals might be most appropriate in other areas (for example, law or religion).

To continue with the science example, in an experimental study where randomization is possible, the warrantability of causal claims is grounded in sampling theory. Sampling theory tells us that when experiments are randomized, influences on the dependent variable are dispersed equally over treatment groups, resulting in a no-difference pretest comparison (that is, randomization achieves comparative equivalence). Comparison groups are employed and pre-post measures are collected. Randomization, comparison groups, and pre-post measures serve as warrants to establish and legitimate the making of causal inferences. Sampling theory goes further and even indicates the strength or force of such warrants by relating sample sizes to variances. Samples should be of a certain size relative to variance to strengthen the claim.

In studies in which randomization is not possible, the warrantability of claims changes. Because of the lack of randomization, and subsequently the associated warrantability that sampling theory provides, the key to strong, defensible claims in quasi-experimentation is the use of pattern matching of causal predictions to the obtained data (verification) and the ruling out of alternative explanations (falsification) (Campbell and Stanley, 1963; Cook,

1993; Cook and Campbell, 1979). As in experimental studies, pre–post measures and comparison groups are used in facilitating causal inferences. However, warrantability is grounded in verification and falsification, more specifically, point specificity (for example, pattern matching in time series and regression discontinuity designs) and in the complexity of causal explanations (for example, multivariate). Point specificity means that if the specific point where an anticipated effect will be observed is clearly identified ahead of time and there is change after this treatment point, then it can be inferred that the treatment had impact. The value of point specificity is that it strengthens the validity of claims. As regards complex causal explanations, the more complex the causal implications, the less likely it is that other explanations exist. The value of complex causal patterns is that they reduce alternative explanations, thereby strengthening claims. As with sampling theory, warrant in quasi-experimental studies also indicates to some extent the strength or force of its warrant. The more alternative explanations that can be ruled out, the stronger the claim.

The reasoning in experimentation is strong because it is based on the long-standing and highly developed area of sampling theory. Such warrant is, for the most part, uncontested and generally accepted as a given. Reasoning that uses this type of warrant is a warrant-using argument (Toulmin, 1964). However, many evaluation approaches are not of this kind. Rather, evaluation approaches tend to be warrant-establishing arguments (Toulmin, 1964). This term refers to warrants that are not uncontested and must be constructed and tried out by application in a number of cases. Here the yet unestablished warrant, as well as the claim, must be legitimated. It is the difference between the "taking of a journey along a railway already built and the building of a fresh railway" (Toulmin, 1964, p. 120). In evaluation, the various approaches seek to legitimate both evaluative claims and warrants.

The development of a quasi-experimental approach is a familiar example of such a warrant-establishing argument in evaluation. "The last thirty years of systematic program evaluation have witnessed two sets of changes . . . in the theory of quasi-experimentation. . . . They concern changes in the intellectual warrant justifying the molar descriptive causal conclusions" (Cook, 1991, p. 116).

In developing quasi-methods for causal inquiry, Campbell began by identifying alternative explanations or causes that random assignment rules out (such as history and maturation). The warrant for causal inferences could be facilitated through falsification. Shortcomings in this warrant led Campbell and Cook to make modifications. One obvious weakness is that the list of alternative causes presumes that it is a comprehensive one. Recognizing this as a weakness, Campbell and Cook later added verification to the original falsification warrant. "Matching specific or complex causal predictions with obtained data became the order of the day" (Cook, 1991, p. 120).

Notice that the warrant was tried out by applying it in a number of cases. Campbell generated his first list of alternative explanations or causes based on his own experiences. Later he identified other new threats through the "reflection of practicing social scientists who had independently identified new threats while on the job" (Cook, 1991, p. 118).

The point is that Campbell and Cook have made outstanding progress in developing the warrantability of causal claims in quasi-experimentation over the past two decades (see Campbell and Stanley, 1963; Cook, 1991, 1993; Cook and Campbell, 1979; Overman, 1988). What contributed to their success, in part, is the fact that they concentrated their efforts at a detailed level. They focused intently on a certain kind of claim (causal effectiveness) and one kind of phenomenon (social intervention programs) conceptualized one way (typically defined as treatment–outcome relationships). Can we get to such an understanding with other approaches used in evaluation practice? Can we better understand and strengthen the different kinds of warrant-establishing arguments in evaluation practice? I believe that the distinction between general and working logic is one means to that end, for it illuminates and characterizes what Campbell and Cook did implicitly so that it can be replicated.

Implications for Practice and Evaluation Theory

New Way to View the Various Evaluation Approaches. The notions of general and working logic are useful to evaluators because they provide a new way to view the various approaches to evaluation. Traditionally, we have viewed evaluation approaches as outlining the purpose of the evaluation (such as formative, summative, or critical), the role of the evaluation (for example, to service management or policy), the role of the evaluator (for example, as facilitator or change agent), the role of the stakeholder (for example, as participatory or representative), the methodological orientation (quantitative or qualitative), the ideological orientation (such as managerial or consumerist), and so forth. This view has resulted in debates such as whether to allow stakeholders to participate in the evaluation, whether summative evaluation is better than formative, whether to include stakeholder views in an evaluation so as to improve the utilization of results, whether to describe or prescribe values, and so on.

These have been informative debates, but they do little to help us with the specifics by which evaluators can legitimate conclusions to stakeholders. Given this understanding of general and working logic, we can now look at these approaches as advancing reasoning on how to construct a particular argument and add other questions to debate. In addition to asking, "What is the purpose of an evaluation?" we can ask, "What question or problem is the evaluation probing?" In addition to asking, "What is the role of the evaluator?" we can ask, "What kinds of claims is the evaluator trying to make?" and "What kinds of warrants will support or weaken such claims?" The general/working logic distinction can help evaluators generate a long list of practical questions about the reasoning used to establish evaluative conclusions in any approach to practice—questions to examine existing approaches advanced by theorists and to raise against approaches put together in everyday practice. The distinction would also be beneficial in expanding how students typically study evaluation approaches in graduate programs around the country.

Illuminates How Evaluative Reasoning Is Influenced. General/working logic is valuable in helping evaluators strengthen the reasoning process they will go through in drawing evaluative conclusions in day-to-day practice because it illuminates the ways in which reasoning is influenced (for example, phenomenon or claim). It makes clear the different features that need to be considered carefully when drawing conclusions in evaluation (such as evidence and warrant). It also shows several ways in which conclusions are open to challenge and criticism. In doing so, it provides evaluators with a series of critical questions by which to examine their practice: "what kind of claim(s) am I trying to make in this evaluation? What authority source does the warrant need to appeal to? How strong is the authority source in supporting inferences drawn from evidence? What conditions would undermine the warrant? How forceful is (or will be) the resulting conclusion?"

In addition, the reasoning pattern presented earlier in Figure 2.5 interconnects such questions in pointing to broader issues. For example, the evidence–warrant–backing relationship that is located on the left side of the argument structure in Figure 2.5 can be viewed as a means for "ruling in" support, and the conditions of exception–qualifier relationship represented on the right side can be viewed as a means for "ruling out" alternative explanations. Using this reasoning pattern, evaluators can ask questions about how an evaluation approach rules in support that strengthens the conclusion and rules out circumstances that weaken the conclusion.

Provides a Practical Concept for Studying Practice and Theory. General/working logic is a practical concept that is useful for studying and comparing what is implemented in practice and proposed in theory because it schematizes evaluative reasoning. It provides a standard means, a unifying construct, for making comparisons across approaches in various fields and settings that have not been easily made in the past. This is important because the "separation of evaluation into distinct subareas, such as program evaluation, product evaluation, educational evaluation, medical evaluation, and others has impeded the development of evaluation theory because similarities across areas are not apparent" (House, 1993, p. 89).

The concept also makes it easier to analyze and critique what is practiced in the field and what is proposed in theory. For instance, the warrant appeals to some authority that legitimizes the inferences drawn from evidence. Examining the kinds of warrants used in practice reveals the nature of the rationality of evaluation as experienced by practitioners. This provides insight into the nature of inferential thinking used by evaluators across diverse settings. Through analysis, progress on the strengthening of the warrantability of evaluative conclusions can be made. Still, the parameters of working logic are ways in which we would expect approaches to vary; thus we can make comparisons between approaches along these four aspects. For example, we might ask, "In what ways is a product the same as a program or a policy? In what ways do phenomena influence the way evaluators justify claims?" The development of the features that describe general/working logic enables us to raise new questions about logical practice. In doing so, we may become clearer about what it means to evaluate something or someone, and what that might mean in various contexts.

Further, having a standard means for comparison could move us away from unproductive comparisons and toward the realization that each approach has its own merit. Rather than saying things such as, "A causal approach has a strong working logic and a connoisseurial approach has a weak one," we can instead ask ourselves questions such as, "If one is making a claim about how students perceive and make meaning, then what kind of warrant would best support inferences drawn from the evidence? What has this approach not considered? What are the actual merits of the approach in light of the kind of claim it seeks to make? What is the best that can be expected of such an approach?" And because warrants confer various degrees of force on the conclusion(s), we are able to examine and categorize types of conclusions and their associated degrees of forcefulness. What kinds of warrants are commonly employed in, for example, a connoisseurial approach to evaluation or in a pluralistic approach? What are the merits of each evaluation approach? What is achievable in one and not in another?

Accounts for Differences Between Diverse Positions. Working logic is valuable in that it is able to account for differences among the diverse positions advanced by theorists and practitioners. For example, it can account for the theoretical incompatibility, noted by Shadish, Cook, and Leviton (1991), in applying the logic of product evaluation, as advanced by Scriven, to program evaluation.

Shadish and others (1991) conducted a comprehensive review and critique of Scriven's scholarship. They contend that the logic of evaluation developed through the study of product evaluation does not fit well when applied to program evaluation (see pp. 83–101). To determine whether the logic fits, I closely examined Scriven's work in product evaluation (Fournier, 1993).

The difficulties in using the logic of product evaluation in program evaluation are a result of blurring the distinction between general and working logic. The objections of Shadish and others are really problems with the variations of detail in which the general logic is followed. In other words, their difficulties are in applying one working logic to another working logic, not with applying the general logic of evaluation to another field, nor with applying a working logic developed in one field to another field. Their difficulties are in using the working logic of a consumer approach to product evaluation as the working logic of a particular pluralistic approach to program evaluation.

Given that an individual working logic is specific to a particular approach to evaluation (that is, particular parameters and reasoning processes), working logic would be expected to transfer to another field if one is willing to accept the parameters of a given working logic. For instance, the working logic of a consumer approach to product evaluation proposed by Scriven can transfer to program evaluation if one is willing to accept the way in which the phenomenon is defined, the kind of questions posed, and so on. A goal-based approach to program evaluation uses this working logic without conflict because it accepts such parameters—it subscribes to conceptualizing a program as having functional properties such as products (program goals). Shadish and others have difficulty with applying this logic because they subscribe to different parameters; they define the phenomenon differently, ask different questions, and so on. But they do agree that the general logic fits across various fields of evaluation. Shadish and others are correct in stating that evaluation logic is not the same for everything, but it is at the level of working logic that such differences arise. The seemingly logical misfit between the working logic of a consumer approach to product evaluation and program evaluation can be accounted for through the conceptualization of two kinds of logic.

Clarifies Professional Identity. When a particular field of inquiry does not have a clear, collective understanding of the nature of the enterprise, it develops loosely and diffusely (Toulmin, 1972). When an area of inquiry lacks an agreed-on understanding about the nature of its enterprise, "the task of arriving at 'rational' judgments is liable—for understandable reasons—to be subtle and debatable" (p. 396). The general logic of evaluation clarifies and defines the nature of the enterprise so that everyone involved is playing the same game.

General logic serves to distinguish evaluation from nonevaluation. In doing so, it clarifies what it means to evaluate something. On this basis it is possible to establish professional identity for the field and a self-concept for evaluators and to shape future developments. This is true because it circumscribes a substantive area of inquiry and orients it from a certain point of view in terms of the perceived nature of its particular enterprise, the nature of the phenomenon undertaken in study, and the nature of its concepts in terms of how members interpret that experience. Professional activities (intellectual and practical) are directed by its goals (well-defined or less specific) and guided by its logic. The discrepancy between what a field aims to achieve concerning some particular phenomenon (its goals) and what it actually can achieve (existing procedures and methods) determines the kinds of problems it seeks to address and the kind of methodological and theoretical developments that need to take place.

Note

1. The warrant is what legitimates the inference one makes when moving from the evidence to the claim. It is the way in which the evidence is connected to the claim. For instance, I state that the new musical playing at the theater is good (claim). To support my claim, I add that I read that it received a good review in last night's newspaper (evidence on which the claim is based). My friend questions me and asks how can I say that. I am not being asked to produce more evidence, but rather to legitimate the inferential leap from the evidence to the claim. I am being asked to legitimate the inference that the musical is good because the newspaper reported it as such. I respond by saying that the reviewer is well-

respected by the performing arts community and that her judgment is highly valued and reliable (warrant). In this example, note that the warrant appeals to expertise. In establishing claims, warrants appeal to different types of authority (for example, because it is the law, because the physician said so, or because *A* is known to cause *B*).

References

Alkin, M. C., and Ellett, F. S. "Development of Evaluation Models." In H. J. Walberg and G. D. Haertel (eds.), *The International Encyclopedia of Educational Evaluation*. Elmsford, N.Y.: Pergamon Press, 1990.

Campbell, D. T., and Stanley, J. C. *Experimental and Quasi-Experimental Designs for Research*. Boston: Houghton Mifflin, 1963.

Cook, T. D. "Clarifying the Warrant for Generalized Causal Inferences in Quasi-Experimentation." In M. C. McLaughlin and D. C. Phillips (eds.), *Evaluation and Education: At Quarter Century*. Chicago: University of Chicago, 1991.

Cook, T. D. "A Quasi-Sampling Theory of the Generalization of Causal Relationships." In L. B. Sechrest and A. G. Scott (eds.), *Understanding Causes and Generalizing About Them*. New Directions for Program Evaluation, no. 57. San Francisco: Jossey-Bass, 1993.

Cook, T. D., and Campbell, D. T. *Quasi-Experimentation: Design and Analysis Issues for Field Settings*. Boston: Houghton Mifflin, 1979.

Eisner, E. W. "Educational Connoisseurship and Criticism." In G. F. Madaus, M. Scriven, and D. L. Stufflebeam (eds.), *Evaluation Models: Viewpoints on Educational and Human Services Evaluation*. Boston: Kluwer–Nijhoff, 1989.

Eisner, E. W. "Taking a Second Look: Educational Connoisseurship Revisited." In M. C. McLaughlin and D. C. Phillips (eds.), *Evaluation and Education: At Quarter Century*. Chicago: University of Chicago, 1991.

Fournier, D. M. "Clarifying the Merits of Argument." In J. Zhao and M. A. Stahl (eds.), *Proceedings of the 1992 Edward F. Kelly Conference*. Albany, N.Y.: Evaluation Consortium, School of Education, SUNY at Albany, 1992.

Fournier, D. M. "Reasoning in Evaluation: A Distinction Between General and Working Logic." Unpublished doctoral dissertation, Syracuse University, 1993.

Fournier, D. M., and Smith, N. L. "Clarifying the Merits of Argument in Evaluation Practice." *Evaluation and Program Planning*, 1993, 17 (1), 315–323.

Hare, R. M. "What is a Value Judgment?" In P. W. Taylor (ed.), *Problems of Moral Philosophy: Introduction to Ethics*. Encino, Calif.: Dickenson, 1972.

House, E. R. *Evaluating with Validity*. Newbury Park, Calif.: Sage, 1980.

House, E. R. "Integrating Quantitative and Qualitative." Paper presented at the American Evaluation Association Conference, Seattle, Nov. 1992.

Kaplan, A. *The Conduct of Inquiry: Methodology for Behavioral Science*. San Francisco: Chandler, 1964.

McCarthy, T. A. "A Theory of Communicative Competence." *Philosophy of the Social Sciences*, 1973, 3, 135–156.

McCarthy, T. A. *Communication and the Evolution of Society: Jürgen Habermas*. Toronto: Beacon, 1979.

McLaughlin, M. C., and Phillips, D. C. *Evaluation and Education: At Quarter Century*. Chicago: University of Chicago, 1991.

Madaus, G. F., Scriven, M., and Stufflebeam, D. L. *Evaluation Models: Viewpoints on Educational and Human Services Evaluation*. Boston: Kluwer–Nijhoff, 1989.

Overman, E. S. (ed.). *Methodology and Epistemology for Social Science: Selected Papers, Donald T. Campbell*. Chicago: University of Chicago, 1988.

Phillips, D. C. *Social Scientist's Bestiary: A Guide to Fabled Threats to, and Defenses of, Naturalistic Social Science*. Elmsford, N.Y.: Pergamon Press, 1992.

Redding, P. "Habermas' Theory of Argumentation." *Journal of Value Inquiry*, 1989, 23, 15–32.

Rescher, N. *Introduction to Value Theory*. Englewood Cliffs, N.J.: Prentice Hall, 1969.

Scriven, M. *The Logic of Evaluation*. Inverness, Calif.: Edgepress, 1980.

Scriven, M. "Product Evaluation." In N. L. Smith (ed.), *New Techniques for Evaluation: New Perspectives in Evaluation*. Newbury Park, Calif.: Sage, 1981.

Scriven, M. "The Evaluation of Hardware and Software." *Studies in Educational Evaluation*, 1990, *16*, 3–40.

Scriven, M. *Evaluation Thesaurus*. (4th ed.) Newbury Park, Calif.: Sage, 1991.

Scriven, M. "Evaluation and Critical Reasoning: Logic's Last Frontier?" In R. Talaska (ed.), *Critical Reasoning in Contemporary Culture*. Albany: State University of New York, 1993.

Shadish, W. R., Cook, T. D., and Leviton, L. C. *Foundations of Program Evaluation: Theories of Practice*. Newbury Park, Calif.: Sage, 1991.

Stake, R. E. "Program Evaluation, Particularly Responsive Evaluation." In G. F. Madaus, M. Scriven, and D. L. Stufflebeam (eds.), *Evaluation Models: Viewpoints on Educational and Human Services Evaluation*. Boston: Kluwer–Nijhoff, 1989.

Stake, R. E. "Retrospective on 'The Countenance of Educational Evaluation.'" In M. C. McLaughlin and D. C. Phillips (eds.), *Evaluation and Education: At Quarter Century*. Chicago: University of Chicago, 1991.

Taylor, P. W. *Normative Discourse*. Englewood Cliffs, N.J.: Prentice Hall, 1961.

Toulmin, S. E. *The Uses of Argument*. New York: Cambridge University, 1964.

Toulmin, S. E. *Human Understanding*. Princeton, N.J.: Princeton University, 1972.

Toulmin, S. E., Rieke, R., and Janik, A. *An Introduction to Reasoning*. New York: Macmillan, 1984.

DEBORAH M. FOURNIER *is associate professor in the Department of Diagnostic Sciences and director of educational research and evaluation, Boston University.*

Combining and weighting (synthesizing) different values, criteria,
methods, measures, and interests depend heavily on content and
context.

Putting Things Together Coherently: Logic and Justice

Ernest R. House

For some time the field of professional evaluation has faced a formidable problem of multiple values, criteria, methods, measures, and interests. After considerable experience and debate, a key development has been that multiple
values and criteria are needed to judge a program's success, that multiple methods and measures should be used to collect data, and that multiple stakeholders might have different interests in the program, so different views and interests
should be represented in an evaluation. Concepts such as critical multiplism
(Shadish, Cook, and Houts, 1986) and multiple stakeholders (Bryk, 1983) are
commonplace. However, this increasing complexity has resulted in a formidable problem: how can results from diverse criteria, methods, measures, and
stakeholders be combined? Often the results conflict with one another.

For example, suppose that in addition to collecting test scores, an evaluator also interviews teachers about an educational program's success. How are
these data combined? Does the evaluator have two conclusions, one for test
scores and one for interviews? Or suppose that in evaluating a science text-
book an evaluator employs 10 different criteria, including readability, fidelity
to science, quality of illustrations, and so on. How can performance on all
these criteria be combined? Or again, in an evaluation of a desegregation policy, an evaluator interviews white and black parents, white and black students,
and school officials. Do all opinions count equally?

The general logic of evaluation, as delineated by Fournier (1993), drawing heavily on Scriven's work, consists of four steps: establishing criteria of
merit, constructing standards, measuring performance and comparing to standards, and synthesizing and integrating data into a judgment of merit or worth.
"Synthesis is perhaps the key cognitive skill in evaluation: it covers everything

invoked by the phrase 'balanced judgment' as well as apples and oranges difficulties" (Scriven, 1991, p. 345). Synthesis is the focus of this chapter, although putting things together occurs throughout the evaluation process.

Following is a suggestion for a general approach to synthesis. The idea is that evaluators work within a specific context to produce an all-things-considered synthesis that provides the most coherence possible from the information available from various sources. More precisely, through substantive deliberation, a process of dealing with particular facts and criteria in context, evaluators can determine the merit or worth of a program (or whatever is being evaluated), and evaluators strive to produce the most coherent account possible, that is, to fit together all the available evidence.

Two key ideas are, first, reasoning about the evaluation in a specific context and, second, searching for an evaluation account that exhibits the most coherence. In general, the best account is the one that brings everything together with the most coherence. However, if the evaluator has achieved coherence by omitting important relevant criteria or information, then the evaluation is disputable. Of course, no account can ever be perfectly coherent, because the evaluator must deal with conflicting criteria, methods, and interests. The world is rarely simple enough to yield conflict-free evaluations. Nonetheless, conflicting criteria and data do not prevent evaluators from arriving at all-things-considered judgments most of the time.

In this conception there is no overall central criterion, method, or interest that the evaluator need appeal to automatically, although one dominant concern may arise in the course of the study. Rather, the evaluator must make do with the specific values and facts within the concrete situation itself, and these limited resources, competently utilized, are sufficient to make quality judgments about the worth of the program under review. Indeed, it is partly the limitation of the context that enables the evaluator to make such judgments successfully. Deliberation about particular facts and criteria in context facilitates sound judgment because the context limits possibilities that might make a determination of worth impossibly complex and indeterminate otherwise.

Faculty Evaluation: An Example

One difficulty in analyzing concepts as broad as coherence and context is that they can mean so many different things. To narrow the argument somewhat, consider a case of how the concepts apply in a particular situation—the evaluation of faculty members for tenure in a research university. Imagine that the issue is whether faculty members should receive tenure and (to make matters precise) that the irascible University Board of Trustees insists that recommendations for promotion and tenure be delivered in rank order. The board is tired of faculty's approving 90 percent of the candidates for tenure.

Of course, research, teaching, and service are the primary criteria for academic merit in most universities. After some consideration, the responsible faculty evaluation committee arrives at the following ranking for criteria of merit:

	Research	Teaching	Service
Faculty member	A	B	C
	B	C	A
	C	A	B

This is a special case of incoherence, where coherence equals transitivity. Although there is consistency within each criterial ranking, when all the rankings are combined, one cannot arrive at a determinate, internally consistent judgment. In transitive distributions, if A is preferred to B and B to C, then A is preferred to C. However, in this case each candidate is preferred to the others, depending on which criterion one uses. Each candidate is first on one criterion, second on another, and last on the third. There are three candidates, one of whom is best on research, another on teaching, and the third on service. This is an incoherent situation from an evaluation point of view, preventing one from arriving at an overall synthesis judgment.

What do we do when this happens? Based on my experience serving on faculty evaluation committees at the Universities of Illinois and Colorado (in which perhaps 500 cases were reviewed), the reasoning works something like this. First, in the early 1980s the University of Illinois was strongly research oriented. Although the criteria were research, teaching, and service (the same as elsewhere), the only thing that counted was research. So that simplifies things considerably. Only the first column counted.

The campus committee of nine professors from different disciplines (no administrators allowed, please) would look at the research records as manifested mostly in publications and grants. The discussion would be about which of these three candidates is best in research. Who has the most publications in the best journals? Who has the best set of references (at least six)? Whose work is most seminal? There would be questions about the quality of the references, with the committee focusing on specific words and phrases. What about the quality of those making the recommendations? What is their standing in the field? Their vitae would be included for consideration. How prestigious a university are they from? (Hopefully, one better than this one.) Were there coauthors? How much of the work did the candidates do? What grants did they receive from where? These considerations, based on data in the candidates' portfolios, provided the basis for the summative ranking on research.

Later in the decade, at the University of Colorado, the balance was different. Teaching had become more important everywhere, and Colorado was somewhat less concerned about research and more concerned about teaching. In principle, both research and teaching were deemed equally important. Service was lauded but not given much weight in such deliberations. That reduces the evaluation to two primary criteria and drops professor C to the bottom rank. The tenure requirement for the University of Colorado reads, "Tenure may be awarded only to faculty members with demonstrated meritorious performance in each of the three areas of teaching, research or creative work, and service, and demonstrated excellence in either teaching, or research or creative work" (*University of Colorado Faculty Handbook*, 1988, p. III-15).

This passage was interpreted as meaning that one must be excellent in either research or teaching but could be good enough ("meritorious") in the other, though not necessarily excellent. If both candidates meet these criteria, for example, one is truly excellent in research and the other in teaching, but only meritorious in the other, the question becomes, "Exactly how good?" If someone is really good in research, this might compensate for performance in teaching, at least to some degree. The same is true for teaching. If one is excellent at teaching, that might compensate for a less-than-stellar record in research. Two candidates would still tie if the judgment were that the committee could not determine differences of degree between them on the basis of detailed evidence in their portfolios.

Here, however, the researcher has an advantage. The implicit scale of excellence for research is more elaborate than that for teaching, perhaps because we have spent more time thinking about research or possibly because there is more inherent variability in research than in teaching performance. With a higher top end, the excellent researcher is likely to be ranked ahead of the excellent teacher on the basis of the empirical evidence available on which to answer the question of exactly how good (unless the data from each are standardized, a procedure not currently in the repertoire of academic evaluation, though student rating data are standardized). So the evaluation is made coherent (transitive) by these considerations, and the committee arrives at an all-things-considered judgment, a transitive ranking of the three candidates, whose future now lies with the board of trustees.

Key Elements

In arriving at a coherent synthesis judgment in this academic setting there are key elements. First, there is a set of reason-giving practices, that is, a set of social-cognitive practices that produce criteria, data, and procedures for deliberation. Academic tradition has evolved methods of judging professors for promotion, including a hierarchy of review committees at the department, college, and campus levels; documents such as vitae with lists of publications; letters of reference from prominent authorities in the discipline; and evidence about teaching, including student ratings and peer observations of classes. Faculty evaluation in academia is both an individual and committee process in which reasons are advanced, argued, and debated, with committee members raising issues or facts missed by colleagues. This is one of the better features of academic evaluation (with excruciatingly long committee meetings one of the worse).

For the most part, these academic practices antedate professional evaluation. By contrast, the set of reason-giving practices of professional evaluators includes the evaluation models and data collection procedures. The evaluation models suggest what is important for the evaluator to consider, and data collection procedures delineate how to collect data in unbiased ways. These are practices the professional evaluator employs. In fact, academia could learn something from professional evaluation, particularly from data collection procedures. Academic methods for collecting data, such as letters of reference, are often biased. Academic evaluation is not professional evaluation.

Nonetheless, once one has criteria and data, reasoning is similar to that in the academic setting. Most differences between academic and professional reasoning revolve around control of potential biases. But both professional and academic evaluators seek coherence in their reasoning by trying to reconcile criteria and data. It would be unusual for either academics or professionals to leave the evaluation in an unresolved, incoherent state, such as that portrayed initially. Of course, sometimes there is no determinate solution, but usually there is.

It is important to note that there is no central criterion that orders the other criteria, thus providing a solution. The evaluators reason with a set of plural criteria and data to produce a resolution. One does not need to introduce other criteria by which to judge or order the other three. Coherence itself is not a criterion for determining academic merit; rather, achieving coherence is an intrinsic feature of the reasoning itself, similar to having criteria. (There are other criteria that could be used to determine academic merit, but that is a different matter.)

A third element of evaluative reasoning is that the context is critical to reaching the synthesis judgment. In this case determination is possible not only because there are criteria for performance (based on the nature of what is being evaluated) but also because the context limits possibilities. If one asked the question, "Which is more important, research or teaching?" in the abstract, there is no way of providing a reasonable answer without supplying some context. However, given a specific context, a determination is usually possible. Not all criteria in a particular setting are equally important, not all criteria are equally fulfilled, and not all weights assigned to criteria remain constant. The limitations of the context enable evaluators to arrive at reasonable judgments.

Finally, these judgments are based on data and evidence to a considerable extent. Evaluative deliberation is both conceptual and empirical. One needs data and evidence with which to reason evaluatively, just as one needs criteria. Substantive (empirical) considerations make critical differences, such as how many publications the candidate has. Facts about the world make a difference. The evaluation cannot be determined without them. Such a view of synthesis reasoning in evaluation is consistent with the general logic (Smith, 1994; Fournier, 1993; Scriven, 1980; House, 1977).

The deliberative process through which one seeks coherence might be thought of in five or so stages (Hurley, 1989). First, the deliberator brings reason-giving concepts to bear on the situation. For the evaluator this means discovering which criteria apply, sometimes an easy task and sometimes not. In the case of academic evaluation, it is too easy, because important criteria may be omitted. Second, the deliberator develops the criterial concepts further, which means defining performance in detail. How is research performance judged, for example? By way of number of publications, quality of journals, grants awarded?

At the third and fourth stages the evaluator examines and explores relationships among criteria and data, perhaps subordinating some to others, perhaps referring to previously settled cases or analogies with other situations to determine the relationships among criteria. These stages are similar to legal judges' analyzing and comparing previous cases, searching for the set of relationships that apply. Finally, one arrives at an overall synthesis judgment. Although there is a general pattern of deliberation, there are different paths for arriving at the solution. (And, of course, the process is far messier than the idealized logic would suggest.)

One might think of the finished evaluation as analogous to a scientific theory. We expect a scientific theory to tell us what to believe given the facts of the way the world is, but we do not expect it to tell us what to believe if the world had been different. Scientists eliminate possibilities by reference to evidence. Similarly, we expect an evaluation to be true for the situation in which it occurred given these particular facts and criteria. We do not expect an evaluation of professors to resolve the issue of the relative importance of research, teaching, and service for all times and places. Nor do synthesis judgments eliminate conflicts. Rather, evaluations are the best judgments we can arrive at in the situation given the conflicts.

It is important to recognize that coherence does not consist exclusively of transitivity. Coherence takes many different forms. I have suggested elsewhere that coherence in evaluation may be achieved partly by generic metaphors that carry implicit and explicit values, so that "target groups," "pipelines," and "goals" are built into the evaluation models. If social programs are understood metaphorically as industrial production, then one can mix machine, assembly-line, and pipeline metaphors so that they cohere even though they do not form a single consistent image, as in "The unreliability of measuring instruments may dilute the difference in outcomes." War and sports metaphors, as well as business and economic metaphors, are prominent in evaluation (House, 1983).

In addition, coherence in individual studies is achieved by devices such as dramatic narratives, storytelling, scene setting, and powerful images that increase the credibility, persuasiveness, and influence of studies (House, 1979). Coherence is an integral feature of evaluation models, of the form and content of studies, and of the deliberative process by which we reason from specific criteria and facts to all-things-considered judgments. In fact, our ability to achieve coherence exceeds our ability to analyze it, as is the case in other intellectual enterprises such as law, science, and drama. But its central importance is demonstrated by how we regard evaluations that we judge incoherent.

Other Synthesis Possibilities

What other possibilities are there for putting disparate criteria and data together to reach judgments? Perhaps the most common method is weight and sum: for example, weight the research and teaching criteria each 40 percent, weight service 20 percent, rate each person on each criterion, multiply, sum the products for each person, and then compare. This has the advantage of arriving at a number, which seems more objective than the intuitive to-and-fro reasoning just described. However, such judgments lack equal subtlety and finesse.

Wise judgments depend in part on being able to shift the weights themselves in some situations. For example, although everyone gets 40 percent for research, sometimes a Nobel Prize winner's research should count more heavily. Or teaching should count more than 40 percent for an extraordinary teacher. In some cases a high degree of excellence should count more than a preset proportion. In the weight-and-sum technique the setting of the weights depends on judgments somewhat removed from the data. Justifying the weights is a problem (Fournier, 1993).

Also, if more variation is inherent in research performance, it will carry more weight in the synthesis judgment arrived at through quantitative techniques than it should (unless standardized). Set weights work better at ensuring that nothing is neglected, a worthwhile consideration that might be handled in other ways. One can require that teaching count in faculty evaluations without necessarily setting weights in advance, although one must make some provision. The finest evaluations may require that the weights themselves shift in some situations and that judgments be arrived at intuitively, although not without discipline imposed through restrictions on deliberation.

In fact, Scriven (1991) contends that the quantitative weight-and-sum approach to combining performances on several criteria is invalid. The technique assumes that results can be fully merged when they cannot be. "Numerical weight and sum assumes linearity of utility (points) across the range of performance variables, which is clearly false" (Scriven, 1991, p. 380). Instead, he proposes a heuristic procedure (as opposed to an algorithm) in which criteria are separated into primary and secondary groups, with secondary criteria employed only after consideration of primary criteria (Scriven, 1994).

Such a heuristic allows primary criteria to play the major role without being overwhelmed by numerous minor criteria, and it still allows secondary criteria to have effects on the summative judgment. For example, in evaluating a science text, one might be concerned foremost with content and with illustrations as a secondary concern. Qualitative weight and sum is an elaboration of this domain restriction procedure (Scriven, 1991). There is nothing incompatible in this procedure with the reasoning process I have outlined, except that it makes some steps in reasoning more explicit.

Another possibility comes from traditional measurement practice. For example, in reviewing methods for combining results, Mehrens (1990) contends that "clinical" methods for combining data are not as accurate as numerical methods. "However, once the judgment about a particular skill has been made, it should be quantified if the judgment about that skill is to be combined with other data. . . . Generally, statistical methods give superior results" (Mehrens, 1990, p. 324). He notes that use of statistical synthesis methods requires several assumptions, such as having a criterion measure, linearity of relationships, or accepting logically assigned weights, depending on which methods are used.

In cases where numbers can be employed, they should be, but in many (perhaps most) evaluation situations they cannot be, and one must use the best judgmental procedures available. For example, combining student question-naire ratings of instructors in large universities can been done in a standardized fashion, thus facilitating the judgments of promotion committees. Integrating data from questionnaires constructed by individual professors would be such a formidable task that it would be almost impossible to use the information.

On the other hand, it is difficult to see how peer reviews of faculty teaching or outside letters of reference can be standardized in their current forms. Peer reviews vary tremendously in content and quality so that assigning set weights to peer reviews of teaching in all-things-considered judgments would be unwise. Some peer observations are brilliant; some are worthless. The same is true of outside letters of reference. If the reference comes from a former adviser, it should not carry full weight. One must look to see what these references con-sist of and weight them afterward. One could also ask outside references to rate candidates on a scale, which might provide useful information to be combined with other information, but such ratings pale beside detailed references.

Moss (1994) has contrasted the psychometric approach to securing test reliability and validity to a hermeneutic approach, focusing on how relation-ships between the parts of an assessment and the whole are treated. In the psy-chometric tradition inferences are based on composite scores aggregated from independent observations across observers and performances. A hermeneutic approach involves holistic interpretations that seek to understand the whole in terms of the parts, that privilege observers who are most knowledgeable about the context, and that involve a rational debate among a community of interpreters, the purpose of which "is to construct a coherent interpretation of the collected performances, continually revising initial interpretations until they account for all the available evidence" (Moss, 1994, p. 7).

Even in an area such as economics, where quantitative indicators are the order of the day, Alan Greenspan, the chair of the Federal Reserve Board, arrives at his decisions about federal interest rates by an intuitive synthesis of informa-tion, which includes both economic indicators and anecdotal information, rather than by a set formula (Bradsher, 1994). This intuitive synthesis prevails in a dis-cipline in which there are sophisticated mathematical techniques, including computer models, numerous indicators, various criterion variables, and the will to use them. However, the all-things-considered judgment comes from the delib-erations of a committee of experts who have reviewed the data intuitively. "His-tory teaches us that the underlying structure of the economy is in a continuing state of flux. Current estimates of key parameters describing the basic relation-ships are based on past experience and need to be viewed skeptically when mak-ing policy for the future" (Alan Greenspan, quoted in Bradsher, 1994).

Within the logic of evaluation all-things-considered judgments with strong intuitive elements are the best we can do in most cases. This reasoning fits the general logic of evaluation, which Scriven calls probative logic. One aspect of probative inference is its iterative nature. That is, a first round of probative inference generates prima facie conclusions, which are tested by further investigation and modified in the light of new data, reaching gradually higher levels of justified confidence but never transcending the possibility of empirical errors. It is largely an implicit logic, just as the grammar of a language is largely implicit, but precise enough for us to be able to create and distinguish grammatical sentences from ungrammatical ones in almost all cases. The tools of inductive argument and critique are analogies, examples, counterexamples, counterexplanations, and contrasts rather than exact rules, and the statements it does use are only rough guides to the truth; they are hints and heuristics rather than exact laws. In probative logic, context is as important as content (Scriven, 1991).

There are other aspects of evaluation (and research) in which the search for coherence in context plays a key role, such as in combining quantitative and qualitative data or interpreting indicators of performance. In these cases the reasoning is similar in form but different in content. The case that is considered further here is a particularly intractable one, the combining of different interests in an evaluation.

Combining Different Interests

Over the past many years (after considerable debate) the inclusion of different stakeholder interests and perspectives has become accepted as a legitimate part of evaluations. This alone has been a major improvement for social justice in evaluation. Assuming that these interests are included, how are they to be combined or weighted? There are several opinions. One is that these values and interests should not be combined, that the evaluator has no authority to arrive at synthesis judgments on such issues. That should be left to the audiences of the evaluation. Another position is that such interests and values can be combined but only in the form of multiple syntheses. That is, the evaluator can rarely arrive at a single conclusion that is legitimate.

My position is that the evaluator can usually arrive at legitimate single (if highly qualified) judgments about the values and interests of stakeholders in an evaluation, although not always. Not drawing conclusions at all may be justifiable under certain circumstances, but this is not the best general practice. Although I am not opposed to multiple syntheses, multiple conclusions are not usually necessary and are sometimes undesirable.

First, how can we balance and weigh such things at all? Consider the parallels with other domains of evaluative reasoning. Professors do not agree on the proper weighting or balancing of research, teaching, and service, nor do university trustees, administrators, or ordinary citizens. Do we therefore send our candidates forward judged separately on research, teaching, and service and encourage university trustees to make the final synthesis? Of course not.

Consider methods for collecting data. Epistemologists do not agree with one another, nor do evaluators, nor social scientists, as to the best data collection methods. Do we send our evaluation reports to our clients and let them decide how they wish to balance test scores against interviews, or correlations with discriminant analyses? Not likely. There is a sense in which evaluators have knowledge and information with which to balance these sometimes conflicting considerations. I believe the same is true regarding stakeholder views and interests if we understand what we are and are not doing.

What we are doing is following appropriate evaluation procedures and guidelines, such as defining criteria and collecting data properly. Then, within a specific context, we are weighing and balancing this information. What we are not doing is assigning weights for all times and places, as in deciding whether research, teaching, or service is most important for all times and places. Nor are we deciding in advance of entering an evaluation that covariance or path analysis or meta-analysis is the best statistical procedure to use. Deciding which procedure is best depends on information obtained in the specific context. It is thus entirely possible to arrive at legitimate, combined conclusions about values and interests.

By contrast, Shadish, Cook, and Leviton (1991) advocate multiple syntheses, reacting in part to my introduction of social justice considerations to evaluation in 1976. They agree that values and interests can and should be included, except that evaluators should arrive at multiple synthesis judgments rather than at single synthesis judgments. "Therefore, one can agree that evaluators ought not to 'cop out' without also agreeing that this is best done by a single summary. One could construct several value summaries, each of the form 'If X is important to you, then evaluand Y is good for the following reasons,' where X is drawn from the interests of different stakeholders or from prescriptive theories" (Shadish, Cook, and Leviton, 1991, p. 101).

The reason for such caution in their view is that there is no general agreement among evaluators, philosophers, legislators, or the public as to proper values or weights. They disagree with using formal prescriptive theories or concepts, such as Rawls's "difference principle" (favoring the interests of the disadvantaged under certain conditions), which "routinely" prescribe the balance of interests among groups.

Evaluators should not use the Rawlsian difference principle as an a priori criterion for every evaluation. Rather, the difference principle provides only one way of conceptualizing situations in which the interests of the disadvantaged are at issue. It is not the only consideration, nor should it be used in all cases to balance interests. But the same is true for using particular statistical methods. The evaluator's conceptual repertoire should consist of several statistical methods, several data collection methods, and several concepts for balancing different interests. These concepts should be employed differentially. Often the interests of the disadvantaged are not a focus.

The way these elements can be combined is through the kind of reasoning illustrated by faculty evaluation. For example, there may be no agreement at the beginning about the proper weights for research, teaching, and service. The balance among criteria may be worked out in the course of the evaluation. Nor is there necessarily agreement at the beginning of an empirical study about how test scores should be weighted against interviews or what statistical technique to use. Pulling these things together is an important part of the study.

(In reacting to this chapter Shadish contends that faculty evaluation is unusual in that evaluators are designated by society to make such judgments, unlike professional evaluators. Also, in his opinion, faculty evaluation is an irrational process. Although I agree that faculty evaluation has unusual features, I believe the professional evaluator is authorized to make such judgments as part of the role. The conditions under which evaluation synthesizing is legitimate is an important topic for further discussion. I also hold out hope for rationality in academic pursuits, perhaps foolishly. After all, the peer review model is the basis for scientific criticism.)

Similar reasoning applies to combining the interests and perspectives of stakeholders. The evaluator does not need prior agreement about the weighting of social justice values to arrive at a reasonable determination. The balance can be worked out in the course of the study through the same reasoning process that works with other concepts and data. What the evaluator does need are specific values, perspectives, and interests to work with, some derived from the stakeholders themselves and some from formal theories, plus agreement about a few tenets of U.S. democracy, such as the idea that all relevant interests should be represented. The problem of combining group interests is similar to combining criteria and data.

For example, consider the Sesame Street evaluation, in which both advantaged and disadvantaged students improved their reading skills but in which the gap between the two groups increased. A utilitarian conception of justice would say that the program was good because test scores were increased for all groups. A Rawlsian conception of justice would hold that inequalities are permitted among groups if the inequality serves the disadvantaged. Hence, the program would be good from that perspective. Only in a strict egalitarian conception of justice would Sesame Street not be a good program, as such a conception would be opposed to any inequalities. Hence, one might arrive at a synthesis judgment that the program is good, but not for decreasing the gap between groups.

Consider Madison and Martinez's (1994) evaluation of health care services on the Texas Gulf Coast. They identified the stakeholder groups as elderly blacks (the recipients of the services), the service providers (mostly white physicians and nurses), and representatives from advocacy groups, such as churches. Each group had different views, with the elderly saying that services were not sufficiently accessible and the service providers saying that the elderly lacked knowledge about the services. Should one construct multiple syntheses based on each group's perceptions, values, and interests? Certainly, all perspectives should be represented, but the evaluators should try to determine which group was correct about the services, and that should be the basis for the synthesis. If the evaluator could not make this determination, then multiple syntheses might be appropriate.

Note that there is no grand determination of the rights of elderly blacks versus those of white professionals. There is only a determination of what is happening with these particular services in this place at this time. The determination of the latter does not depend on resolution of the former. Context and specificity make evaluation possible. Of course, informed evaluators would be aware that whites traditionally have attributed social program failures to the internal personal characteristics of blacks and also that these elderly people might not be knowledgeable about services. There is no need to resolve the difference before the evaluation is conducted.

Let us push the limits of the argument with an extreme example, as philosophers do. What if the evaluation determined that the medical services provided in Texas contained strong racist elements? Surely that aspect of the program would be condemned by the evaluators. Evaluators wouldn't say, "The program is good if you are a racist, but bad if you are not," which would be making different syntheses for different groups with different values. Evaluators would question the values themselves. And if the evaluators found that services were much better for men than for women, shouldn't they say that this is undesirable?

Presenting if–then value statements for each audience seems inadequate. Evaluators should not accept stakeholder values and interests at face value. Rather, the values and criteria themselves must be examined. Of course, in some cases a determination may not be possible because the information is not available and multiple judgments will be necessary. It could be that the evaluator cannot determine what is happening even after a thorough study.

However, I do not want to exaggerate my differences with Shadish, Cook, and Leviton's position. We agree that the values and interests of important stakeholder groups can and should be included in an evaluation, that the evaluator can and should make syntheses, and that the evaluator should not use formal theories of justice in a routine, a priori manner. The difference is about how many syntheses the evaluator is authorized to present. (In addition, their descriptive valuing versus prescriptive valuing scheme seems inconsistent. An evaluator constructing multiple syntheses of values and interests seems necessarily normative, not descriptive.)

They have overstated the case for social disagreement. Although U.S. citizens do disagree about many things regarding democratic values, there are large areas of agreement, as has been demonstrated empirically (Hochschild, 1981; Schuman, Steeh, and Bobo, 1985). Although philosophers, legislators, and the public disagree, they disagree within frameworks of overall agreement about fundamental democratic values, for example, that all legitimate interests should be represented in a democracy. Disputed issues, such as abortion, are dramatized by media attention, whereas agreements are not.

Evaluation in a Cognitive Democracy

Formally, the assertion that evaluators should not or cannot balance contending interests seems similar to the one for academic promotion. If substitutions are made in the table for faculty evaluation, it is evident that coherence and transitivity are not permissible in this situation, in this view.

	Equality	Excellence	Entitlement
Interest group	A	B	C
	B	C	A
	C	A	B

In other words, this is an intransitive situation that should not or cannot be resolved rationally by the evaluator. If one prefers equality, then the interests of group A should prevail; if one prefers excellence, then the interests of group B should dominate; and so on. In this way of thinking there is no rational resolution, but only preferences in the eye of the beholders, depending on group values or interests. Evaluations become means through which personal or group preferences are realized.

However, such value issues can be resolved rationally. Evaluators can reason with specific criteria and facts in context. The result is not a determination of equality compared to excellence in U.S. society. That determination is beyond the powers and duties of the evaluator. Rather, the task is to balance the views and interests of elderly recipients and service providers in Texas, given what has happened there. No doubt, such a synthesis requires data collection and complex deliberation. But the determination need not depend on one central, overriding set of values agreed to in advance.

Nor does the resolution require that the evaluator act as philosopher-king (queen), telling everyone what to do. One can imagine two extreme positions: a value-free evaluator making no value judgments at all, or an evaluator-philosopher-king deciding everything arbitrarily on the basis of his or her personal values. However, we need not go from one to the other, any more than we need go from "no values allowed in science" to "anything goes." Rather, there is a considerable range of possibilities for handling values between these two extremes.

The single-synthesis position is not that of the philosopher-king who decides what is right arbitrarily and then acts on it. Rather, the evaluator is constrained by the rules and procedures of professional evaluation. Nor is the evaluator's role to make decisions for legislators. Those with political authority make their own decisions based on evaluation studies (we hope) and other sources of information. (Nor is there empirical evidence that policy makers have been overwhelmed by our studies.)

The use of formal philosophic theories, such as Rawls's (1971) theory of justice, can serve to inform and critique our positions but need not be used to determine judgments in every evaluation, or how certain interests should be weighted in advance of the study. Rawls's notion of weighting the interests of the disadvantaged in a certain way offers the evaluator conceptual possibilities, as do various statistical methods for analyzing data. No single theory of justice or value is accepted universally, nor is any statistical method or data collection procedure. Statistical and social justice concepts need not be universally endorsed to be useful. Admittedly, considerations of social justice and balancing interests are not as well developed in evaluation as statistical methods, but that is because efforts have not been made to do so.

Believing that evaluators cannot or should not weight and balance interests within a given context is a miscasting of the logic of evaluation. It suggests that human choice is based on nonrational or irrational preferences, not rational values, and that these things cannot be adjudicated by rational means. It implies a view of democracy in which citizens have irrational preferences and self-interests that can be resolved only by voting and not by rational means such as discussion and debate. A cognitive version of democracy, one in which values and interests can be discussed rationally and in which evaluation plays an important role by clarifying consequences of social programs and policies, is much better than a preferential version.

Unfortunately, evaluators have inherited a reluctance to deal with social justice and value issues from value-free social science, which was shaped during a period of history when social scientists were persecuted for their political beliefs. Social scientists avoided value issues, claiming they could only determine causal claims. In fact, only a few decades ago many thought evaluation of social programs to be an impossibly arbitrary task. Some still do.

Two other criticisms of social justice considerations are worth noting. Shadish, Cook, and Leviton quote two evaluators who also contend that we should not work with such concepts. "I am very suspicious of those who say they are speaking for the poor or disadvantaged when they themselves are not poor or disadvantaged. It strikes me that the highest form of elitism occurs when persons unchosen by the disadvantaged say that they speak for the disadvantaged or they say that they take the disadvantaged's interests into account. Let us be concerned, but let us remember that we can speak only for ourselves" (Kenny, 1982, pp. 121–122, quoted in Shadish, Cook, and Leviton, 1991, p. 51). "Most modern evaluators are concerned with the fairness, justice, and ethical conduct of the government. However, most of this work is done by contract from the government and for the government. There is little opportunity to negotiate agreements, and all audiences are assumed to be represented by this legitimate authority. For the evaluator to challenge this except in clear legal and ethical violations of conduct would be foolhardy" (Wortman, 1982, p. 124, quoted in Shadish, Cook, and Leviton, 1991, p. 51).

Apparently, Kenny's objection is against paternalism. My position is that the interests of disadvantaged groups should be included in evaluations where they are major stakeholders, along with other interests. If anything, I am acting as a spokesperson for evaluators, asserting that they have a responsibility to seek out the views of the powerless and include those in evaluations, not for evaluators to say what the views of the powerless are without investigation. For example, if one contends that the interests of females be considered in evaluations of mathematics education programs, is that paternalism? I doubt that women would agree that it is.

Wortman reflects the anxiety of many practitioners. Because the evaluator is in the service of the client by contract he or she cannot challenge the client's authority. How would one obtain more contracts? It is not that the evaluator cannot make the judgments, but that he or she dares not. Scriven's lamented value-phobia, the reluctance to make value judgments, is often derived from power-phobia, fear of those in power. These are overblown, more projected fears of the possible than the likely, although the issue is open to empirical investigation. I believe the government even seeks advice on these issues.

As for the contention that "all audiences are assumed to be represented by this legitimate authority," clearly this assumption is false. "Only 20 percent of Americans trust the government to do the right thing most of the time, down from 76 percent 30 years ago" (Gore, 1993, p. xxix). The American people do not believe that the government fully and reliably represents their interests. Evaluators cannot afford to believe that the government is an infallible guide to people's interests, important as official views are. If such were the case then there would be no need to collect the views and interests of stakeholder groups. One would attend only to government officials. There is a critical distinction between government and civil society, demonstrated by the fact that scientists do not produce the findings that officials want. Nor should evaluators.

The last argument against balancing various interests is that U.S. society is pluralistic; hence, interests should not be balanced but left to stand on their own. No doubt, American society is pluralistic. But as philosopher Thomas Nagel has said about the fragmentation of values in modern society, "Our capacity to resolve conflicts in particular cases may extend beyond our capacity to enumerate general principles that explain those resolutions. . . . What we need most is a method of breaking up or analyzing practical problems to say what evaluative principles apply and how. . . . Radical disagreement about the basis of ethics is compatible with substantial agreement about what the important factors are in real life" (Nagel, 1979, pp. 135, 139, 141).

That is what we try to do in evaluation. Evaluative logic and reasoning help us see how to do it. There is nothing in democratic pluralism that argues against reaching evaluative conclusions. Certainly, we should recognize the pluralism of society, but we also need ways of putting values and interests together again rationally. Disaster awaits a democratic society that cannot do so.

References

Bradsher, K. "Greenspan Says the Fed Uses Anecdotal Guides." *New York Times,* Aug. 11, 1994, p. C-2.

Bryk, A. (ed.). *Stakeholder-Based Evaluation.* New Directions for Program Evaluation, no. 17. San Francisco: Jossey-Bass, 1983.

Fournier, D. M. *Reasoning in Evaluation: A Distinction Between General and Working Logic.* Unpublished doctoral dissertation, Syracuse University, 1993.

Gore, A. *Creating a Government That Works Better and Costs Less: The Report of the National Performance Review.* New York: Plume Books, 1993.

Hochschild, J. L. *What's Fair: American Beliefs About Distributive Justice.* Cambridge, Mass.: Harvard University Press, 1981.

House, E. R. *The Logic of Evaluative Argument.* Center for the Study of Evaluation. Monograph no. 7. Los Angeles: University of California, 1977.

House, E. R. "Coherence and Credibility: The Aesthetics of Evaluation." *Educational Evaluation and Policy Analysis,* 1979, *1* (5), 5–17.

House, E. R. "How We Think About Evaluation." In E. R. House (ed.), *Philosophy of Evaluation*. New Directions for Program Evaluation, no. 19. San Francisco: Jossey-Bass, 1983.

Hurley, S. L. *Natural Reasons*. New York: Oxford University Press, 1989.

Kenny, D. A. "Review of *Evaluating with Validity*." *Educational Evaluation and Policy Analysis*, 1982, *4*, 121–122.

Madison, A., and Martinez, V. "Client Participation in Health Planning and Evaluation: An Empowerment Education Strategy." Presented at the American Evaluation Association, Boston, Nov. 3, 1994.

Mehrens, W. A. "Combining Evaluation Data from Multiple Sources." In J. Millman and L. Darling-Hammond (eds.), *Teacher Evaluation*. Newbury Park, Calif.: Sage, 1990.

Moss, P. A. "Can There Be Validity Without Reliability?" *Educational Researcher*, 1994, *23* (2), 5–12.

Nagel, T. *Mortal Questions*. Cambridge, England: Cambridge University Press, 1979.

Rawls, J. *A Theory of Justice*. Cambridge, Mass.: Harvard University Press, 1971.

Schuman, H., Steeh, C., and Bobo, L. *Racial Attitudes in America*. Cambridge, Mass.: Harvard University Press, 1985.

Scriven, M. *The Logic of Evaluation*. Inverness, Calif.: Edgepress, 1980.

Scriven, M. *Evaluation Thesaurus*. (4th ed.). Newbury Park, Calif.: Sage, 1991.

Scriven, M. "The Final Synthesis." *Evaluation Practice*, 1994, *15* (3), 367–382.

Shadish, W. R., Cook, T. D., and Houts, A. C. "Quasi-Experimentation in a Critical Multiplist Mode." In W.M.K. Trochim (ed.), *Advances in Quasi-Experimental Design and Analysis*. New Directions in Program Evaluation, no. 31. San Francisco: Jossey-Bass, 1986.

Shadish, W. R., Cook, T. D., and Leviton, L. C. *Foundations of Program Evaluation*. Newbury Park, Calif.: Sage, 1991.

Smith, N. L. "Investigative Methods in Outcome Evaluation Studies of Psychological Interventions." Paper presented at the American Psychological Association, Los Angeles, Aug. 1, 1994.

University of Colorado Faculty Handbook. Boulder, Colorado, 1988.

Wortman, P. L. "Review of *Evaluating with Validity*." *Educational Evaluation and Policy Analysis*, 1982, *4*, 22–25.

ERNEST R. HOUSE *is professor of education at the University of Colorado, Boulder.*

Logic of evaluation has significant implications for practical methodology.

The Logic of Evaluation and Evaluation Practice

Michael Scriven

This chapter sets out some definitions of common terms used in talking about evaluation and then identifies a set of crucial problems about the nature of evaluation and its components. Two of these problems are addressed here. The first is the fundamental problem of how evaluation is logically possible at all. The second is the recommendations problem: how an evaluation can provide support for recommendations, by contrast with mere evaluative conclusions about whatever is being evaluated. Some implications of each of these problems for evaluation practice are then spelled out.

Basic Concepts

The phrase *logic of evaluation* is used here to refer to the specific principles of reasoning that underlie the inference processes in all and only the fields of evaluation. The general logics of inductive, deductive, and statistical inference, although widely used in evaluation, are not part of the logic of evaluation as the term is used here, as there is nothing evaluation-specific about them. However, particular applications of those general principles may be specific to the practice of evaluation and hence fall under the logic of evaluation.

For convenience, I now make some distinctions that are not clearly implied by the common use of the terms. Fields of evaluation, where, of course, evaluative claims are the main findings, are distinguished by their evaluative subject

Criticisms are most welcome and should be e-mailed to scriven@aol.com or sent to P.O. Box 69, Point Reyes, CA 94956, or faxed to (415)663-1913. Thanks to Deborah Fournier for some valuable comments on an earlier draft.

matter. Some of the more common fields involve the evaluation of programs, proposals, personnel, products, performances, and policies, although there are a dozen other recognized fields of evaluation, ranging from the appraisal of real estate to applied ethics, literary criticism, and the evaluation of evaluations (meta-evaluation). Fields are distinguished from areas: areas are distinguished by their nonevaluative subject matter, the preexisting application discipline to which evaluation is being applied. Typical areas are education, health services, and roadtesting. Some areas can require the application of many fields of evaluation—education involves program and personnel evaluation (and several other fields), whereas road-testing simply involves product evaluation. Evaluative claims are those that attach evaluative predicates to a subject such as those from the list of fields, including a claim that a property is valuable or a program is no longer highly ranked. An evaluative predicate is one drawn from the vocabulary of grading, ranking, scoring, or apportioning—or one that is not definable without recourse to that vocabulary. Finally, evaluation types are approaches used by various evaluators or one evaluator: true experiment, advocate/adversary, goal-achievement, goal-free, naturalistic, and the like. Evaluation type is closely related to evaluation method but includes some approaches that are more ideological and less clearly defined than what are normally thought of as methodological approaches, such as empowerment evaluation.

It is useful to make a rough distinction between two levels of problem in the logic of evaluation, as in deductive logic. The first level involves defining, clarifying, and relating the key concepts via axioms and definitions—the foundations level. Clarifying the foundations includes relating these concepts to other concepts from neighboring disciplines. The second level involves developing what might be called the working principles, roughly the equivalent of useful constructions and theorems. In the work of the surveyor, for example, the analog would be the geometric construction for identifying the midpoint of a line, and Pythagoras' theorem. These provide a key procedure and a key working principle for the surveyor. This is the applications level, but it is still a level within the logic of evaluation or logical methodology. Beyond that, of course, there is the practice of evaluation and all the practical wisdom that goes with it; that is not the domain of logic but of practical methodology. In that domain, corresponding to the practical wisdom the field surveyor acquires with experience about the use and handling of equipment, we can locate generalizations about the right mix of quantitative and qualitative approaches for certain types of problem, the advantages and limitations of goal-free evaluation, how to do useful cost analysis, the relation between the probability of conclusions and their credibility, and so on.[1] The difference between the applied logic of evaluation and evaluation methodology is essentially the difference between conclusions that can be established on logical grounds and those that are based on experience and empirical evidence. The latter may therefore vary somewhat from field to field within evaluation, whereas the former must apply across all fields. Evaluation theory, by contrast with the logic of evaluation, can deal with topics or issues from either the logic or the practice of evaluation. It will generate normative theories in the first case and either normative or descriptive theories in the second case, depending on the topic.

In evaluation the foundational concepts requiring definition include evaluation itself, defined here as the systematic investigation of merit, worth, and significance; the definition of those terms; and the identification and definition of its four distinctive basic operations: ranking, grading, scoring, and apportioning.[2] These all need to be distinguished from closely related and contrasting concepts. Evaluation has to be distinguished from near-synonyms such as assessment (and two dozen others that are less similar), on the one hand, and from substantially different concepts such as monitoring, needs assessment, measurement, explanation, and description on the other; bias needs to be distinguished from commitment, formative evaluation from summative evaluation, and so on. Extensive discussion of these matters has been provided elsewhere, so they are not elaborated here (see Scriven, 1991, 1995). Instead, I concentrate on a selection from the most important logical problems that evaluation faces, problems about the logical constructions that it appears to require and the logical principles that should govern it. These problems are so serious for evaluation, and the attention so far paid to them so slight, that the discipline is running a considerable risk of building on sand, or at least failing to move in the optimal directions for development and influence.[3] It is hoped that this chapter will be a stimulant for criticisms and improvements by others as much as a contribution by the author.

The four key issues in the logic of evaluation on which some comment is provided here, perhaps the four most important problems it faces at the moment, appear to be the following.

Fundamental Problem

The fundamental problem is a construction problem: the problem of whether and how one can get from scientifically supported premises to evaluative conclusions. In the history of thought and science, this kind of inference has been widely believed to be impossible because of two alleged impossibility proofs. The first of these is best known from Hume's work, and it was later reinforced by G. E. Moore's "open question" argument. It is now possible to see that these arguments are without merit—but to see this required some relatively recent developments in logic. This problem is often seen by practitioners as rather remote from the real world of evaluation practice they inhabit, where it seems odd to suggest that every conclusion they reach may be illicit; indeed the problem cannot, realistically speaking, threaten all of them. However, the problem does raise questions that threaten the validity of many, although by no means all, of their conclusions. The specter of the impossibility proofs also explains much of the opposition to the notion of scientific or objective evaluation, and laying it to rest would therefore do much to improve the standing of evaluation in the community of disciplines and the support of leading scientists for doing and following up on evaluations.

Synthesis Problem

The synthesis problem is the problem of when and how one can integrate several subevaluations (or scores on different dimensions of performance), each referring to a different dimension of the performance or qualities of a particular evaluand[4]—or each referring to different components of the evaluand—into an overall evaluative conclusion. Systematic approaches to this problem—that is, those that do not simply consist of "experienced judgment"—usually involve the use of intuitive weight-and-sum algorithms, of which all the usual ones are invalid. Some complex efforts at a systematic approach have recently been made by social scientists under the heading of multi-attribute utility technology (MAUT), but these efforts are almost totally irrelevant to the practice of evaluation (they require data that are usually unavailable) and have serious problems of validity. (I have recently discussed this problem elsewhere, so it is bypassed here.[5]) Note that the synthesis problem we are talking about here concerns performance synthesis, problem 2A, and is not the problem of combining multiple value profiles on the part of a set of consumers into an overall or optimal value profile of "the market" or "the affluent consumer," and so on. We could call the latter the problem of values synthesis, problem 2B, and it has received more attention from social scientists (such as Kenneth Arrow[6]) without producing very useful conclusions. It does deserve more attention, although it is not as fundamental, for two reasons. First, it does not arise with the single consumer or highly congruent groups of consumers (or in many other cases), whereas the performance synthesis problem will still arise in virtually all of those cases. Second, a resolution of this problem is not needed to come to specific evaluative conclusions that are useful for individuals and groups; some of the reasons for this are given below in an example about product evaluation.

Recommendation Problem

This is the problem of when it is and is not possible to infer from an evaluative conclusion about, for example, a program (and perhaps its components), to a recommendation as to what should be done with the program (or a component). This problem has scarcely been recognized, let alone solved. It is usually supposed that such inferences are obviously valid in principle; in fact, they are invalid in principle, although sometimes defensible in particular circumstances. Because of this dependence on circumstances, it is essential to spell out exactly what assumptions are being made if recommendations are to be put forward on the basis of an evaluation. An indication of the seriousness of this problem is that unless it can be solved, essentially all research on implementation is invalid. This is so because implementation can only be of recommendations, recommendations require validation that is additional to the validation of the evaluation, and no such validation was provided in any of the implementation studies with which I am familiar.

Indicator Problem

For the most part, indicators in the social science literature are accessible (that is, measurable or observable) correlates of—but not conceptually part of—the criterion variables. (Sometimes there is a suggestion that they have to be correlates of causal variables that partially control the criterion, but this is not the general usage.) Evaluators have made considerable use of indicators of one kind or another as criteria of merit. For example, the widely used checklists for evaluation of teachers via classroom observation are usually based on research that shows that certain observable variables are correlated with improved student performances (in the so-called process/product research). However, this particular use of correlates as criteria of merit is totally illicit, as is their use in most other areas of evaluation, such as in the evaluation of programs and organizations. If such correlates were licit criteria of merit, then the use of black skin color, because it is positively correlated with crime rate, could be used as a criterion of (negative) merit in hiring. The reasons against this are not just ethical and legal, but also scientific and statistical. Perhaps the main reason this "fallacy of statistical surrogation"—the use of correlates instead of primary criteria of merit (such as the pupil's acquisition of valuable learning due to the teacher's activities)—has not been recognized, or certainly not stressed, is that the scientific sin here is one of omission rather than commission. (That is, the inference from the generalization to the particular case is licit when and only when we have no detailed job-relevant information about the evaluee, that is, where we have failed to gather any track record data for the evaluee, such as in cases that do not meet minimum standards for serious personnel evaluation.[7])

There are some significant consequences from this point in the logic of evaluation. For example, the use in personnel selection of tests that are not work samples or simulations is illicit. Once again, there are special circumstances such as emergencies or the practical impossibility of obtaining other data, where the use of indicators as criteria of merit can be justified; and there are times when very low intersubject variation in properties makes it less dangerous. The use of a brand name (and model number) in some product evaluation is perhaps the most common example of the latter case; but note the difference between using the indicator as a search heuristic (acceptable) and using it as a criterion of merit (unacceptable in general). Of course, the intersubject variation in personnel evaluation is very high. We sometimes, although not often enough, recognize the invalidity of even highly correlated indicators, for example, in blind reviewing for journals, in the derogatory phrase *guilt by association,* and in preventing juries from having access to prior criminal records of defendants. I have extensively discussed this topic elsewhere (Scriven 1987, 1990), so I will not repeat the arguments here.

Deborah Fournier has raised the interesting question whether this position on indicators threatens "theory-based evaluation," which appears to use theories about the operation of the evaluand to identify indicators for evaluative purposes. It seems possible that this would lead to indicators, which could be used only as criteria of merit in the absence of primary criteria, but the matter needs further study.

Other Problems

One might add to this list of leading problems an equal number that also deserve serious consideration, whose listing may stimulate contributions to their solutions, as well as additional suggestions from readers: the explanation problem of clarifying the relation of evaluation to explanation, the issue on which "theory-based evaluation" commits to one answer; the needs problem, which requires defining needs and needs assessment; and the parameter problem of identifying the parameters that define a particular evaluation problem, to the point where an appropriate design can be suggested (there are at least a dozen of these[8]). To these we should add problem 2B, the values synthesis problem, which is important in certain cases of policy evaluation.

Recommendation Problem

Of the two problems to be addressed here, it seems preferable to begin with this one because it has immediate practical consequences for all evaluators and because it can be handled without any significant excursion into technical logical vocabulary. The effort here is to establish its credentials as a serious problem and introduce a sketch of a treatment.

To understand the recommendation problem and its importance, one needs to see that it constitutes the focus of a fundamental, albeit often unrecognized, disagreement about the very nature of evaluation, especially program evaluation. Program evaluators fall into three groups with respect to the question of when their task is completed: we can call them the minimalists, the purists, and the activists.

The minimalists think that evaluation consists of determining the facts relevant to a decision maker's decision, such as determining what a certain group of children learned as a result of the intervention being evaluated (outcomes) or what the experience was like (process). They believe that placing a value on these facts or perceptions is something best left to the client. A sociological problem with this view is that it marks out no new territory for evaluation, because determining the facts is just traditional applied social science, and "giving the view from the inside" is a more recent (minority) view of legitimate social science. A pragmatic problem is that the client is not in a good position to do objective assembly of a very complex dataset—referring to process and outcome results—into an overall evaluation.

The minimalist view, of which Marvin Alkin is a well-known advocate, is very powerful in the field of program evaluation, as can be seen from the fact that at least two journals with the word *evaluation* in their titles publish little except reports of empirical outcome studies. As mentioned, the notion of evaluators who never draw evaluative conclusions is not only paradoxical, but it makes the notion of an autonomous profession of evaluators redundant. They are no more than relabeled social scientists, as indeed many social scientists think is the case.

The paradox—amounting to an absurdity—is unavoidable, so minimalists should not refer to themselves as evaluators; they do no evaluation, although they do some very valuable footwork for evaluations. The redundancy is suspect, because evaluators can exist and perform a useful and distinctive function in many other areas, such as personnel and product evaluation. And process evaluators, looking at programs in terms of, for example, equity or legal use of funding, work in the social sciences without much dependence on traditional social science. To think that the evaluator's role, as something distinct from data gathering, is impossible or inappropriate in program evaluation is surely just a case of being unclear on the concept.

The purists think that evaluation goes much further than minimalism, but not as far as the activists want to stretch it. They believe it does not end until the merit, worth, or significance of the evaluand has been determined. To determine merit of course requires more than merely determining outcomes or examining processes; it requires weighting the importance of each dimension of merit and then combining those results with all the relevant values, notably needs assessment data and whatever ethical, legal, or scientific standards apply. The purist thinks that the conclusion of an evaluation is a claim about comparative or absolute merit, or worth, or significance, the choice among these depending on the needs of the client. This stakes out a territory beyond that of empirical social science, but one where credentials can be established, as clearly the legitimate and skilled practice of evaluation in this sense goes back several thousand years. Beyond that point, that is, with respect to excursions into recommendations or instructions, the evaluator does not see a place for the evaluator unless he or she is also the decision maker or a remediation specialist.

The activists think that the purists are giving up much too soon, making just the same error of improper limitation that the purists condemn the minimalists for making. Activists believe that the main function, or at least a very important function, of evaluations is to generate recommendations.

The argument here is that the best first approximation is the purist position, but with a couple of significant concessions in the direction of the activists without making that an acceptable primary perspective.

Logical Problems with the Activist Position

The fundamental problem with the activist position is that it is logically unsound. From conclusions about the merit or worth of a program it is generally impossible to draw further conclusions about what should be done by the decision maker. Suppose that the decision maker is a funding agency that has asked the evaluator to look at program X, now up for refunding. The agency makes clear that it feels it still has a commitment to the population targeted by X. Both the purist and the activist agree that we can at least conclude the following:

> C1. Program X represents the most cost-effective and ethical way to meet those needs of its target population that it addresses within the financial resources of the funding agency.

What recommendations follow from this? The most likely candidate is the following:

> R1. Continue to fund X.

But this clearly does not follow. The inference depends on many missing premises. The target population has other needs besides those addressed by X; the agency might now feel it is important to pay some attention to those. The knowledgeable program officer who is an essential part of any further support of X again may have just departed. Funds may have declined since the evaluation was commissioned. And so on and on. All of these circumstances are matters about which the evaluator knows little or nothing, and about which he or she has made no systematic determination of importance. It is careless and presumptuous to propose R1 as if it is a finding from the evaluation. The evaluation finding is C1, and that represents useful input to the decision makers. They are then in a position to make a finding about appropriate action based on many considerations including the results of the evaluation.

Here is a more extreme example (not that the first example is something often encountered). Suppose that the conclusion about merit and worth points in the opposite direction:

> C2. Program X seems clearly to be greatly inferior to several alternatives and in fact seems to be almost completely ineffective.

Surely we can at least infer this recommendation:

> R2. Do not provide further funding for X.

No. The inference in R2 is in general invalid. There are many contextual factors that could make it appropriate, perhaps imperative, to continue with X. The facts about the program do not override these, and hence it does not follow from the evaluation of the program that it should not be refunded. Such factors include cases where the alternatives to X will require expensive installation and training time, for which funding is not available; cases in which there is powerful external political support for X, so that the agency may have to compromise by refunding X in order to do the best overall job with its total program portfolio, or perhaps even to survive or itself get refunded; and cases where it is imperative to avoid violent contention among board members, who are sharply divided about X, because much more important issues confront the agency. Although decisions such as the decision not to refund X are sometimes improper, they are not always, let alone necessarily, improper.

But surely none of these possibilities alter the fact that the evaluator is entitled to, indeed must, say that he or she recommends actions R1 or R2, while understanding that recommendations can be and sometimes should be overruled. To do less would surely be to ignore the plain implications of the results of the evaluation. On the contrary, not only should the evaluator not recommend R1 or R2, but it is simply illicit to suggest that they are implications of the evaluation at all. To produce them is just to produce conflict and confusion within the agency and its clientele, who, seeing the contrast between what the evaluator recommends and what the agency does, think that something improper has occurred. But usually what has occurred is that the evaluator has transcended the legitimate role of an evaluator, and that is always confusing. The confusion is compounded by the fact that many clients expect recommendations but do not provide all the additional information that would be required to make them possible. Of course, even the client cannot provide the expertise that is also required.

Suppose one were to argue that a proper reconstruction of the evaluator's recommendation would show it to have an implicit premise of the form "other things being equal." This reconstruction is often described as saying that R1 or R2 are conclusions with prima facie force, not categorical force (or that they are prima facie implications of C1 and C2). There is indeed a place in the logic of evaluation for the notion of prima facie inference, as shall be seen in the following discussion of the fundamental problem. But that place is not here. One might as well say that a jury's conclusion of guilt should have a recommended sentence attached to it. Judges are in possession of facts, experience, and knowledge of context, prior records, and law that juries do not have. Conclusions about guilt do not justify even prima facie assertions about sentences (with rare exceptions, such as where the sentence is legally tied to the finding of guilt). The bottom line is that the strongest legitimate conclusion from the evaluator is the conclusion about the merit or worth of the evaluand. The consumer and the client know that this conclusion has a certain relevance and value to them in the course of decision making, but the rest is up to them.

The confusion created by the opposite assumption is not confined to the client and the clientele. Evaluators and researchers have also been seriously confused by the fallacious suggestion that evaluations should always or normally end in recommendations. Most of the fuss in the evaluation literature about the frequent failure of clients, especially government clients, to "implement evaluations" was based on a confusion between evaluations and recommendations. Evaluations cannot be implemented. They can be taken into account, but they are not the only source of information relevant to decisions—including ethical and rational decisions—about the future of programs. There is little evidence that evaluations are not generally taken into account, to an appropriate degree, except where they have become irrelevant since the evaluation was commissioned, other factors having overdetermined the decision. It would be extraordinarily difficult to discover such cases through scientific investigation—it certainly can't be done with the usual blunt instrument designs—but once in a while they turn up, occasionally through confessions. Such cases are often cases where the client's intent was nefarious—to get a justification for a hatchet job, which the evaluation did not supply; or the converse cases, where a justification for favorable treatment was sought, which the evaluations did not provide. Those few cases are important because they reveal the true values of the client. They are sometimes highlighted by firing the evaluator but it is much more common for them to be simply concealed by burying the evaluation or by going through a charade of treating it as input and overweighting "other considerations" for not going in the direction it points.

Micro- Versus Macro-Recommendations

The error of jumping to recommendations is not confined to recommendations about the disposition of programs—what might be called macro-recommendations. Evaluators often make recommendations of a less global kind about what should or should not be done to improve various components or aspects of a program (micro-recommendations). These, too, are usually not implications of the evaluation but jump beyond the evaluative findings, although the subevaluations on which they are based are well founded. The missing premises required to bridge the gap typically include assumptions about the absence of interactive effects from this action on other aspects of the program and assumptions about the remedial effect of the suggested changes, something about which the evaluator is rarely an expert.

It is perhaps easiest to see this by using an example from product evaluation. A good automobile road tester has considerable expertise as an evaluator, and this expertise entitles him or her to come to conclusions about the merits of a car along certain dimensions (handling, reliability, and so on) and, by putting these together, to overall conclusions about the merit of the car (comparatively or absolutely). Additionally, it is legitimate for the road tester to draw evaluative conclusions about certain components, such as the brakes, the headlights, and the wipers, and the legibility of the instruments. These are conclusions about the extent to which these components perform the appropriate functions, and the evaluator has plenty of experience on the basis of which it is possible to say how the level of quality of these components rates against state-of-the-art standards, against minimum acceptable standards, and against the norm, in the price or functional class of vehicle being tested. Many evaluators who have defended the importance of recommendations as part of the evaluator's task in formative evaluation have failed to realize the enormous value of these subevaluations as feedback to the manager or developer looking for guidance toward improvement. Recommendations are not the only path to improvement, and micro-evaluations are usually more legitimate than any recommendations, whether macro or micro.

The moment the road tester begins to make specific recommendations, whether to the manufacturer or to the consumer, the path of justification becomes much rockier. To recapitulate the previous point, the macro-recommendation that everyone about to buy a new small econo-sedan should buy an X—or that no one interested in a new small sedan should buy an X—simply presumes too much about contextual variables. Should they buy it even if they really dislike its looks? If they have to wait a month for delivery? If it lacks a ski pass-through in the back seat, although they are avid skiers? The macro-recommendation is an assertion aimed at a large group of people who vary considerably in respects that are relevant to purchasing. By contrast, the conclusion that this is the best, or worst, car in its class, averaging across the needs of many consumers or idealizing various types of consumers from a mixed population, swings the focus back to the car, identifying it as the best of its type. Naturally, consumers look at their idiosyncratic needs and preferences in the process of applying this evaluative conclusion to their own case. Aesthetics and small-group needs are rightly set aside, or given a passing reference, in professional evaluation of functional artifacts.

For such reasons, road tests often conclude with cautious remarks such as, "This car should be given serious consideration by anyone looking for an economy sedan," which is a recommendation but not much more than a rephrasing of the evaluation. It is a truism that anyone considering the purchase of an expensive product should (rationally speaking) look at relevant facts and evaluations. People making decisions about the future of programs should consider the results of evaluations of those programs. That is trivial: it is always true, but it does not tell decision makers that they should do one or the other of the things they can elect to do. It is a long way from the specific recommendation to refund or withdraw support, and it is these specific recommendations that are often thought by evaluators to follow from the evaluation. I will come back to this in a moment.

First, however, I will follow the product example through to the micro-level. The argument is the same as at the macro-level. It is proper to draw any of the following conclusions about the headlights in the Lexus LS400. They are weak; too weak for safety in senior citizens, whose sensitivity to light goes down by 50 percent; well below the state-of-the-art standard for luxury cars, set by the BMW 750il with its xenon lights; or below the norm for luxury cars, defined, say, as those over $40,000. But the suggestion (micro-recommendation) that one should put xenon lights in the LS400 is unjustified (under heavy loading conditions, they require load-leveling rear suspension to avoid blinding oncoming drivers, which would price the 400 out of its market). One could of course recommend that "something be done about the lights," but that scarcely qualifies as the kind of recommendation that clients seek.

Diffuse Versus Specific Recommendations

This leads to a general point. One of the reasons why it is tempting to think that evaluations entail recommendations is that they can reasonably be said to imply this kind of phantom recommendation, essentially a mere restating of the negative recommendation. So we need to distinguish between these recommendations and recommendations of defined feasible actions. I will call these two types of recommendation diffuse and specific. In these terms, "Interior storage space needs to be increased" is diffuse—just a translation of a poor evaluation into a ghost of a recommendation—whereas "Door pockets should be added" is specific. Another example of a diffuse micro-recommendation would be, "Some way should be sought to improve fuel consumption." This is, so to speak, a way of pointing out the evaluative conclusion (that fuel consumption is not very good by the relevant standards) in the direction of the manufacturer. Because the manufacturer is always looking for ways to improve fuel consumption to avoid the federal penalties on high corporate fuel consumption and already knows the fuel consumption of the model line courtesy of the federally required tests, this is essentially an empty recommendation. An example of a specific kind of micro-recommendation of a highly relevant and potentially useful kind is, "In order to improve fuel consumption, the present intake fuel injection system should be replaced with throttle-body fuel injection." Although it is a much more useful kind of recommendation, it does not follow from the evaluation in a road test. It might of course follow from an evaluation of the options available to the manufacturer, if this were done by an engineer rather than a road-tester, and if the evaluator were given a mass of data not available to road-testers. Analogously, program evaluators are not, per se, social engineers. If they acquire the kind of detailed knowledge that the theory-driven approach suggests, then they have become engineers; but this is more than most evaluators can achieve except by severely limiting the range of programs they can evaluate. There are big differences between health programs and education programs in terms of local expertise, and between types of health programs and types of education programs. Furthermore, there are serious grounds for skepticism as to whether there are reliable program theories in many of these areas.

Particularly with respect to micro-recommendations (for example, increase the size of the glove box, or lighten the clutch pedal), there are many problems about such changes that the evaluator is rarely in a good position to estimate: problems about its cost, about increased complexity of the production engineering of the change (and hence a risk of reduced reliability), about legal liability, and about consequential costs (larger glove box means less leg room, and so on). It seems clear that the evaluator per se should report on the merit of the glove box and the clutch pedal effort but should keep to that. Such remarks have their own significance for actions by the manufacturer and consumer but in each case have to be fitted into a complex composition that will always require some compromises. In general, making evaluative remarks is all that is legitimate. If, however, it seems more useful, the symbolic recommendation that adds nothing more specific may be chosen as the way to express the same point.

Middle Ground: Where Specific Recommendations Can Be Justified

The gap between the purist and the activist can be bridged in two ways. The first is by expanding on the point just made about the value of focused (micro) feedback for the improvement effort. The second is by spelling out four types of situations for which the evaluator can legitimately add recommendations.

Evaluator Has Expertise at the Micro Level with Respect to This Kind of Evaluand

For example, say that the road-tester is also an automobile engineer. In these cases, the recommendation is then dependent entirely on this expertise and is an add-on to the evaluation. Essentially, the evaluator is saying, "As an evaluator I can show that X needs improvement, and as an engineer it seems to me that Y is the way to improve it, so I recommend Y." The problem with this, as can be seen by looking at what goes wrong with accreditation of professional schools, is that the second part of it is often more a matter of opinion than of expertise, but it receives extra and illicit weight because the first part is provable. In road-testing, this problem can be put by saying that the car was designed by a team of competent engineers, so the opinion of one more, who happens to have been the road-tester, cannot be automatically accepted simply because the road test shows the need for further improvement of this component. Nevertheless, there are some cases in which the contribution from the evaluator with a second area of expertise is useful, provided both sides are clear that the recommendation requires a separate justification from the evaluation and a great deal of extra information not usually available to the road-tester. The evaluation shows that something needs to be improved, but as to how this is to be done, the evaluator becomes just another micro-level consultant.

There are one or two interesting cases in which the gap requires little bridging. For example, in evaluating the self-evaluation process in a program, it takes no extra expertise to recommend, for example, that the program make some use of external evaluators, because evaluation is one's own field of expertise. In another kind of case, in which one discovers improper hiring and promotional practices that discriminate against, say, women, by penalizing longer time-to-doctorate without taking any account of maternity leaves, one not only can but must recommend a change in the process, because ethical transgressions are stand-alone faults. However, the way in which that change is to be brought about is beyond the expertise of the typical evaluator.

Evaluator Has Full Decision-Related Data and Expertise at the Macro Level with Respect to This Kind of Evaluand

For example, say the evaluator works for a foundation and has acquired extensive knowledge of its overall values and resources. After evaluating a particular program, which turns out to have little value, the evaluator is able to see that nothing in the foundation's decision environment provides an overriding reason for retention. Again, the point here is that two areas of expertise are involved, and challenging the second one is not the same as challenging the first. The evaluator may simply be wrong about the political ambiance but completely correct about the evaluation of the program. (Of course, so may the foundation's decision makers, and the situation is complicated by the fact that they may not have a single view.)

Needs Assessment Data Indicate a Homogeneous Population

For example, say the client is an individual who asks for a recommendation, such as which graduate program to enter or which car to buy or whether to hire Jones, Smith, or Robinson. In that situation it is possible for a good evaluator to run a needs assessment on the client that will focus the evaluation to the point where it implies a recommendation. This case extends to the case in which the client asks for an evaluation of options for another group, not including the client, but the other group is homogeneous with respect to the relevant variables. For example, they are all terminal cancer patients with essentially the same life expectancy and the question is what analgesic is best for them. This situation is rare in program evaluation.

Client Asks for an Evaluation of the Decision Alternatives

This is a further step beyond the two previous cases. It is much harder than just evaluating one of the entities that is involved in the decisions, roughly because it involves becoming a macro-expert in the decision space where the client is operating, as well as doing an evaluation of the various evaluands floating around in that space, not to mention thinking up new alternatives. As in case 2, the bottom line is that there are two levels of evaluation involved, and the validity of the inferences and data for each should be considered separately.

Evaluator Wants to Convey a More Specific Estimate of Worth

Even when evaluators lack full knowledge of the decision space for the decision makers who are their ultimate customers, they will sometimes feel uneasy about the limited vocabulary available to them to express worth and may use the recommendations as a way to convey a sense of their estimate. If recommendations are used to serve this function, it should be (but often is not) understood by the evaluator that they are very likely not to be implemented due to factors beyond the evaluator's ken. Thus "This program should be discontinued" has to be read as meaning "Nothing that we know about could justify continuance."

Conclusions

The step to specific recommendations requires separate expertise and certification (of data and inferences) beyond the skills required for an evaluator. It should not be taken, even if requested by the client, without demonstrating that expertise and providing that certification. The purist is right to say that evaluation expertise of itself does not justify this step (very special cases apart); the activist is right to say that we should try to bridge it when we can (that is, when we have the expertise); the cynic is right to say that all too often the evaluator is seduced by the client, or precedent, or the wish to help, or an overoptimistic view of his or her own expertise into thinking that it is a small and natural step from the evaluation to the recommendations.

In case it appears that the preceding argument makes a strong case for using evaluators with expertise in the field of the evaluand, this may be an opportune moment to stress that such expertise nearly always carries with it a lack of experience in looking at the field from the outside, such as from the consumer's point of view, or the point of view of another field competing with the first one for resources, or the point of view of someone without connections to the old boys' network in the field. And the time it takes to acquire the local expertise usually means less skill acquired in general-purpose evaluation. A good principle of practical methodology suggests that teaming local expertise with general evaluation expertise is the best solution.

Fundamental Problem

This is the problem of providing a legitimate basis for inferring to evaluative conclusions: that is, a basis other than arbitrary evaluative premises. This means using either premises that are factually established, theorems from deductive logic or mathematics, or commonly accepted definitions. Although this problem threatens the validity of all evaluative conclusions, logically speaking, few evaluators are seriously concerned about it. Like mathematicians informed that there is a crisis in the foundations of mathematics, they feel that this is a philosophical crisis rather than a real one, and their common sense tells them that it will be resolved in their favor. This is true in a sense; much of their work will be left intact, such as impact data collection. But it is also true that the exact way in which the issue is resolved will have some significant consequences for practice, notably in defining the range of legitimate activities for the evaluator. Solutions to the recommendation problem, for example, depend on how the fundamental problem is solved. It is also important that resolving the issue in a convincing way is likely to have a significant effect on the status of evaluation among the company of disciplines, because, in the eyes of many others, the specter of invalidity has long haunted this field.

The problem is simply explained. We can, by the usual process of scientific observation and inference, reach empirical nonevaluative conclusions. We can also, by deduction, reach mathematical and logical conclusions from common definitions, and from the axioms of mathematics and logic, which are themselves either definitions or self-evident in some strong sense. It appears that none of these premises or conclusions are evaluative propositions, and none of these inference rules bring them in, and hence it appears that one cannot reach any evaluative conclusions from such proofs. Thus it appears that the only way to reach evaluative conclusions is to add evaluative premises. These will, it appears, be arbitrary, because no evaluative premises can themselves be established by these processes of logical, mathematical, or scientific inference. And if the premises are arbitrary, one might equally well adopt contrary premises and derive contrary evaluative conclusions. Hence no evaluative conclusions can be established that deserve to be treated as any more true than their denial; that is, no evaluative propositions can be established that meet the minimum requirement for true propositions. This is a development of the Humean argument, and its conclusion is what I will call the dismissive view (of the status of evaluative claims).

The main weakness in this line of argument—and in Moore's rather different one leading to the same conclusion—is that it is based on grossly oversimplified notions of definition and inference, notions that have been refined since Moore's time. That there is something wrong with the arguments is clear enough if we hold firmly on to our common sense, because of their reductio ad absurdum (overkill) nature. The absurdity is clear enough from, for example, the fact that according to the dismissive view all published product evaluations are guilty of a logical fallacy, although they proceed by good inference from facts to evaluative conclusions. Their missing premises are the common conceptions of the common products they evaluate, such as knives, radios, and houses, plus a general understanding of the concepts of merit, worth, and significance—that is, what it means for something to be better or worse among its kind, more or less valuable or significant. But seeing that the dismissive argument and view are unsound is one thing; seeing why they are unsound takes a little more work. The extra work is worthwhile because it shows exactly what the mistakes were that led to the view, and once seen, these are deprived of any residual charm. I will approach the refutation by reconsidering the classical views of definition and inference. The sequence is important because the reanalysis of definition is the key to the reanalysis of inference. This is not easy reading for those who do not remember their logic courses, but it is important and applies to almost all evaluands and evaluations.[9]

Definitions. The concept of a definition in traditional logic—still to be found in most current texts—was that it consisted of an equivalence between the defined concept, X, and a set of terms, C1, C2, and so on, that could be substituted for that concept without loss of meaning. This meant that (1) each member of this set of Cs was a necessary condition for the concept, often put by saying that they are "individually necessary,"[10] and (2) the set as a whole was jointly sufficient (that is, it is a contradiction to say that all are present but the concept does not apply). This was indeed true of concepts in mathematics, from which the notion came, and it is true of many neologisms at the time of their introduction. But it is a misrepresentation of the situation with most everyday concepts (such as apple or friend) and all the major concepts in science (temperature and so on), as well as most of the more complex concepts in the dictionary. These are cluster concepts, that is, ones whose meaning is learned and explained by reference to a number of criteria that do not constitute a set that is jointly sufficient and individually necessary. The set of criteria for X has three weaker properties:

1. *Although some of the criteria may be necessary conditions for X, in many cases none of them have that status.*
2. *Although some subsets of criteria from the complete list must be sufficient—for otherwise we could never know when to apply the concept X—they are sufficient only for all practical purposes, but not with logical certainty.*

That is, it is conceivable, although unlikely, that such a set, which everyone thinks is sufficient to show that X is present, is really not sufficient. Moreover, the complete list of criteria is often very long, often not known to anyone (in the sense that anyone could list it when asked), often contains functional accounts of the way the term is used (for example, with terms such as *and* or *large* or *good*), and often contains contradictory components. Of course, at most one of the contradictory components will be present in any particular case. Contradictory components, familiar enough in the definition of disease entities, are usually of the form C5 or (not-C5 and R). For example, disease X is characterized by symptoms C1 and/or C2, and so on, and by C5 (a mottled pink skin rash) or not-C5 (no rash but small subcutaneous nodules (C6)).

3. *Although the set of criteria is not sharply defined, it is loosely distinguished from other factors (known as indicators) that may often be found in conjunction with the defined concept by the fact that criteria are, and indicators are not, sometimes put forward and defended as part of the meaning of the concept.*

For example, sunrise is a preoccurring indicator for sunset but not a criterion for it. The line between criteria and indicators is obviously not sharp, and it shifts with time and our growth of knowledge. Criteria also vary in weight at a given time and over time, and there is some agreement on gross differences in weight among experienced users of the concept, but nothing like a complete or precise account of these weights.

This imprecise relation between a concept and its meaning applies just as much to the key concepts in science as it does to well-known slippery notions in everyday talk, such as *democracy* or *equality*. This can be seen in the various definitions of temperature that have reigned in the history of thermodynamics. The definitions did not encapsulate the whole meaning of the concept; they were just leading criteria that it was convenient to enshrine in a definition for a while, until the theory to which they were connected began to look a little shopworn. Then we called into service some of the other criteria that had been occupying a background role for a while, often embedded in a theory, and elected them to definitional status.

Many of us puzzled over the allegedly empirical status of Newton's Laws of Motion, especially the third law ("For every action there is an equal and opposite reaction"), thinking that it looked very much like a definition of *reaction,* but in fact its use in the parallelogram of forces construction in statics gives it some indirect empirical content (that is, buildings constructed on that basis tend not to collapse). Hence *reaction* is a concept that can be defined criterially but not in terms of a classical definition. This is indeed the most common situation with deeply theory-embedded concepts in the sciences: whatever definition was used to introduce them originally, their present meaning is more complex, and usually only specifiable in terms of criteria.

Inference. What is the nature of the inference from a set of apparently adequate criteria to the concept itself? As stated above, although this is sometimes a deductive step (when the term is classically definable and we have listed all the criteria that occur in the classical definition), in practice it is often just a very reliable but not absolutely irrefutable inference. Yet it is more than that, too, because the criteria (and their relations) are, collectively, all there is to the meaning of the concept. So the inference is at least nearly as strong as inference via a classical meaning rule, for example, from *three-sided plane figure* to *triangle*. That is, it is nearly as strong as deduction (sometimes it is deduction), and it is not just an empirical inference from indicators that are connected by mere correlations with the concept. This kind of inference is a leading type of what has been called "probative inference."[11] It is neither deduction nor plain inference from observed generalizations, and it is the key to handling the logic of evaluation.

Payoff Time. Suppose we are evaluating a cooking pot. If we understand the meaning of the term, then we know what it is for (its purpose), as this is something whose definition essentially brings in function.[12] Knowing what it is for and knowing what it means in general to do something well (or badly), we can quickly generate a comprehensive list of dimensions along which a cooking pot can be ranked for merit: leakproof, able to withstand the heat of fires and flames (and preferably ovens), not easily cracked or split by typical kitchen tools and treatment, preferably able to withstand being dropped, preferably corrosion resistant and inert to chemicals contained in food or generated in the cooking process, preferably easy for most cooks to lift, preferably with lifting handles that stay cool, preferably with a lip that allows pouring without spilling, and so on. Someone who knows the meaning of the term without ever having used a cooking pot will recognize that this list covers most and perhaps all of the dimensions along which pots vary in merit. If we add the desirability of low cost, we have a checklist for evaluating worth or value. If we add aesthetic considerations, we start to consider the pot as an art object or as in part an art object, and we find that that dimension allows only poor objectivity.

Hence, from the common meaning of the term and the common meaning of the concept of merit, we can generate enough criteria of merit to allow a solid inference from high performance on each or most of the dimensions on that list to the conclusion that the pot is a good (or bad or better) one. Determining whether the performance is high involves determining standards for *high* and then applying them. The standards mainly or entirely emerge from the definition (for example, *absolutely leakproof* is as high as one can get on that dimension). That is a definitional matter, involving the definition of a term with a common meaning, and hence not vulnerable to the charge of arbitrariness. Applying these standards is an empirical matter, and hence not vulnerable to those embracing the dismissive thesis (the value-skeptics).

It will take knowledge of the market prices to infer to good value, and knowledge of the range of pots available to infer to most, although not all, judgments of relative merit. But that further knowledge is empirical knowledge, readily obtainable and intersubjectively testable, like the most reliable scientific knowledge.

Now the objections to inferring from facts to values have been eliminated. The inference is probative, not deductive or classical inductive, but good enough to bet the farm on, and it is based on understanding two concepts—pot and merit—in the common language, which cannot be classically defined, only criterially defined.

What comeback from the value-skeptics is possible? The premises that brought in the values are at most of the form, "The more leakproof a cooking pot is, across a range of several days' use, the better it is." Or "The lighter a cooking pot is, within the range that current materials make possible, then, other things being equal, the better it is."[13] These are provably true, and the proof comes from an understanding of the concepts involved and perhaps to some extent an understanding of the context of use. To challenge these as arbitrary statements, which could just as well be denied as accepted, is to be speaking another language, not our native tongue.[14]

Conclusions for Practice

The discussion of inference here shows that the logic of evaluation at most requires identification of the criteria of merit for the evaluand, not a classical definition of either the evaluand or merit.[15] This suggests that the effort to set out the criteria of merit being used should be made more explicit in many evaluations. Doing this in the case of program evaluation, for example, makes it rather obvious that one cannot plausibly restrict the criteria of merit to those based on the goals and objectives of a program. It is necessary to brainstorm other possible effects and functions that may turn up as side-effects, just as in the evaluation of cooking pots one may thereby think of the fact that pots are typically more useful if other pots can nest inside them, thus greatly reducing the space required for storage, or of the fact that they are more useful if they have a handle made to facilitate hanging the pot, say, on a hook. This approach to side-effects should complement the usual one of looking for them blindly or through open-ended questions in interviews.

The bottom line of the inference section here is of course to establish not only the possibility but the relative ease of rock-solid inferences from unchallengeable definitional and factual premises to evaluative conclusions. This type of premise is what consumer product evaluation has always used, and it is the type that the professional program evaluator and personnel evaluator should be using.

The discussion of definitions, apart from serving as the basis for the introduction of probative inference, also emphasizes the possibility of providing entirely satisfactory definitions of complex concepts without submitting to the tyranny of classical definitions. It is only necessary to indicate as many criteria for the term as possible, just as in evaluation we try to list as many criteria of merit as possible. It is not crucial that we find them all, but it is sufficiently important that we find nearly all of them that we should try out our attempts as hypotheses, in this case hypotheses about meanings, so the trial should involve a sample of experienced users of the terms.

The section on recommendations also has implications for practice, which are spelled out there in some detail, but can be summarized in the leading sentence of the concluding section of that part: The step to specific recommendations requires separate expertise and certification (of data and inferences) beyond the skills required for an evaluator. Although some evaluators have this further expertise, many and perhaps most of them are compromised as evaluators by the ties they develop in the course of acquiring the expertise. Hence, evaluators should never feel that they are on balance weaker as evaluators if they lack local expertise about the particular type of evaluand. What they lose on the swings they make up on the roundabouts. However, they should make an effort to form an evaluation team with a locally expert evaluator or use local experts as consultants to the evaluation (two very different approaches).

Overall, it is hoped that the chapter shows how the logic of evaluation is not only of intellectual importance as the backbone of the discipline of evaluation but worth studying for its significant implications for practical methodology.

Notes

1. A longer list of principles, for one field of evaluation, is proposed in Scriven (1993). A good example of a relatively undiscussed problem in this area is disclosure, that is, the problem of how much and when the external evaluator should show drafts or final evaluation reports to those who are evaluated (see Scriven and Kramer, 1995).
2. There is a rough relationship between this set of concepts and the fundamental concepts in the logic of measurement: nominal, ordinal, interval, and ratio scales. However, only two are closely equivalent (ranking provides an ordinal scale on merit, worth, and so on, and the usual type of scoring supposedly, although in fact rarely, provides a ratio scale).
3. Three of the examples here are construction problems, and construction problems sometimes prove impossible. A good example of this in geometry is the problem of squaring the circle, on which a vast amount of time was wasted before an impossibility proof was discovered. We need to decide what constructions are and are not possible in evaluation, a task for the logic of evaluation.
4. The term *evaluand* is used here to refer to whatever is being evaluated, such as a program, performance, person, proposal, product, or policy. *Evaluee* is used to refer to any person who is, is part of, or is a stakeholder in an evaluand, such as the staff of a program being evaluated. (*Evaluatee* has some currency as a term for the person evaluated in personnel evaluation.)
5. The background of the problem is discussed in some detail, and its crucial importance is illustrated by reference to a number of familiar examples, in "The Final Synthesis," in Scriven (1994). A crude version of a technical solution, using a qualitative weighted sum approach, is in Scriven (1991). It is much improved in the fifth edition (1995) and is also available by request to those sending a stamped self-addressed envelope. These references contain a justification for the remarks about the invalidity of the usual weighted-sum approaches and the irrelevance of MAUT.

6. Arrow's impossibility theorem has some connection with this issue. It is a trivial result that, contrary to various popular interpretations, has no implications for the nonfeasibility of democracy.

7. When we do have track record data, we "know too much" to be able to use a generalization that applies only to a population defined more generally. This is clear in the limit case, where we have a paradigm of a good teacher, that is, one who scores outstandingly on all primary criteria but who goes against the research-based indicators. (We know there are many of these teachers because the correlations are quite modest.) Should we mark them down because they do not follow the rules? This would obviously be unjust and, on consideration, absurd, because the correlations were established based on an independent criterion of good teaching, that is, doing well on the primary indicators. We can hardly use the indicators to invalidate the very examples from which they draw their own, secondary legitimacy.

Suppose blue-eyed golfers are statistically better than brown-eyed ones. That fact can be used to make a weak inference to merit as long as one does not also have the testimony of good witnesses as to the golfer's average number of strokes per round in the current season. At that point, it is ridiculous to argue that that testimony should be downweighted against information that someone has blue eyes. The situation is not improved by using the elegance of someone's swing instead of eye color, that is, a criterion that has some plausible connection with merit. Once usable evidence about primary criteria of merit is available, the evidence about secondary criteria (correlates of primary criteria) becomes worthless.

The only exception occurs for a generalization that relates to a subclass defined by common evidence about primary criteria. If all we know about Janet is that she is a teacher who uses high time-on-task, we can infer that she is more likely to be successful than Robert, about whom all we know is that he scores low on time-on-task. But if we also know that Janet has mixed references from previous supervisors, whereas Robert's are uniformly good, we cannot offset that by weighting Janet's style in her favor. She lost on the primary indicators and is no longer part of a population of teachers about whom we have only secondary indicator data. We can now use her time-on-task in her favor only if we also have a generalization that says teachers with weaker references are better than those with better references if they exhibit high time-on-task. In short, so-called research-based indicators cannot be used once we have a typical dossier, which includes evidence about primary criteria of merit (knowledge of subject matter, communications skills, assessment skills, ability to relate to peers and parents, and so on); that is, they are of no use in practical cases.

8. There is a first try at this in Scriven (1989), which is condensed in the entry on Evaluation Parameters in *Evaluation Thesaurus*.

9. The following analysis is a development of the one originally set out in Scriven (1959). That account represented an attempt to render more explicit Wittgenstein's analysis of meaning. The entry under Logic of Evaluation in Scriven (1991) provides more detail but is slightly less accurate.

10. Saying that a criterion is necessarily connected with a concept is to say that it is a contradiction to assert that the concept applies to something but that the criterion does not. However, contrary to another classical notion, a contradiction is not sharply distinguishable from a highly implausible or almost meaningless claim. Nevertheless, it remains a useful notion because there are plenty of clear cases of contradiction even if there are some debatable borderline cases.

11. The legal term *probative* is defined in the *Oxford English Dictionary II* as "having the quality or function of proving or demonstrating; affording proof or evidence; demonstrative, evidential." The term was introduced to logical theory in Scriven (1987a). Probative inference also covers cases of inference to a conclusion that is established beyond a reasonable doubt but not to a conclusion that represents only the best interpretation of the data, the balance-of-evidence criterion.

12. The *Oxford English Dictionary II* defines *pot* as "a vessel of cylindrical or other rounded form, and rather deep than broad, commonly made of earthenware or metal (less commonly glass), used to hold various substances, liquid or solid, for . . . cooking or boiling." Of

course, this isn't a classical definition; we would have no trouble in calling a square pot a pot, or a fireproof plastic container a pot. In fact, for many years cooking pots in some cultures were commonly made of bark, but that does not show the definition to be incorrect, owing to the insulating function of the term *commonly*. In the list that follows, the term *preferably* serves an insulating function.

13. Actually, one needs only a weaker claim: "Cooking pots that have many of these properties are better than those with few of them." To establish at least one evaluative conclusion, one needs only "Cooking pots lacking all these properties are not good," or the converse.

14. I have omitted all discussion of Moore's open-question argument, which raises no new issues. It works only if we assume that the only legitimate form of inference to evaluative conclusions has to be deduction and the only legitimate form of definition has to be classical. Once one sees that only probative inference and criterial definitions are required, here as in all nonartificial discourse, the force of the argument evaporates.

15. As a matter of interest, there are a few cases where the dismissive thesis is completely wrong on its own terms because there are a few arguments with evaluative premises that are definitional truths and not arbitrary. Hence there are a few arguments that can legitimately proceed by using these propositions, along with factual claims as the other premises, and reach nonarbitrary conclusions. For example, the proposition "murder is wrong" is true by definition because any case of killing for which there is a justification is not a case of murder in the commonly used sense of that term. Hence, we can establish the conclusion that X is a murderer by using this premise plus factual premises that rule out all of the finite list of justifications for killing. John Searle has used the premise "deliberately breaking a promise is wrong" for the same kind of argument. Some hard fighting has gone on in the philosophical literature to avoid this crack in the wall between facts and values, but most would agree that it has not weakened Searle's case.

References

Scriven, M. "The Logic of Criteria." *Journal of Philosophy,* 1959, *56,* 857-868.

Scriven, M. "Probative Logic: Review and Preview." In F. H. van Eemeren, R. Grootendorst, J. A. Blair, and C. A. Willard (eds.), *Argumentation: Across the Lines of Discipline. Proceedings of the Conference on Argumentation.* Dordrecht, The Netherlands: Foris, 1987a.

Scriven, M. "Validity in Personnel Evaluation." *Journal of Personnel Evaluation in Education,* 1987b, *1* (1), 9–23.

Scriven, M. "The Logical Specifications of an Evaluation." *Australasian Journal of Evaluation,* 1989, 2 (1), 31–38.

Scriven, M. "Can Research-Based Teacher Evaluation Be Saved?" *Journal of Personnel Evaluation in Education,* Fall 1990.

Scriven, M. *Evaluation Thesaurus.* (4th ed.) Newbury Park, Calif.: Sage, 1991.

Scriven, M. (ed.). *Hard-Won Lessons in Program Evaluation.* New Directions in Program Evaluation, no. 58. San Francisco: Jossey-Bass, 1993.

Scriven, M. "The Final Synthesis." *Evaluation Practice,* Oct. 1994.

Scriven, M. *Evaluation Thesaurus.* (5th ed.) Newbury Park, Calif.: Sage, 1995.

Scriven, M., and Kramer, D. "Risks, Rights, and Responsibilities in Evaluation." *Australasian Journal of Evaluation,* Jan. 1995.

MICHAEL SCRIVEN is an attention-span challenged scholar who has spent large amounts of time in departments of mathematics, philosophy, psychology, and education; and in developing the new disciplines of technology studies, computer studies, evaluation, and informal logic. He is now director of the Evaluation & Development Group, a small consulting company in Inverness, California.

Informal logic in philosophy and evaluation share considerable common ground and can offer each other various opportunities for meaningful cross-fertilization that can lead to advancements in theory and practice in both fields.

Informal Logic and Reasoning in Evaluation

J. Anthony Blair

In this chapter I briefly describe the field of informal logic and outline some of the major issues in reasoning that are of concern to informal logicians. These issues are of similar concern to evaluation practitioners and theorists. As I point out in the discussion that follows, there are some interesting parallels in the analyses of reasoning in the two fields, thus suggesting that they could learn much from one another.

Why is attending to the reasoning involved of any importance to the practice of evaluation? A full answer to this question will emerge, but there is a quick and easy response available at the outset: cognitive psychology confirms the common-sense hypothesis that metacognition improves performance of first-order cognitive tasks. An understanding and awareness of the operations involved in carrying out any exercise of intelligence, be it simple computations in arithmetic, sophisticated statistical analyses, or "synthesizing and integrating [evaluative] data into a judgment of merit or worth" (House, this volume), will lead to carrying out those operations more efficiently and with greater sophistication. It is the cornerstone of any sound process of inquiry.

What Is Informal Logic?

Informal logic is the moniker that has come to be used for a set of issues, related to the interpretation and evaluation of arguments and reasoning, taken on by a group of philosophers beginning in the 1970s. The field is defined by a set of

I wish to thank Deborah Fournier and two anonymous reviewers, whose criticisms and suggestions on an earlier draft were right on target, and helped me enormously to focus this paper.

common problems rather than by a single theory or theoretical outlook.[1] I will focus on those informal logic problems and proposed solutions that seem to me to have a possible connection with the reasoning used in the practice of evaluation, and in particular with some of the matters discussed in the first four chapters in this volume. This brief inventory of the ways informal logicians have been going about understanding and evaluating reasoning will, I hope, give evaluation practitioners an abbreviated but concrete sense for possible applications of informal logic to their practical and theoretical concerns. First, some distinctions must be made between the terms *inference, reasoning, implication,* and *argument.*

Some Necessary Distinctions. Informal logic originally dealt with interpreting and evaluating reasoning or arguments, but distinctions have been drawn between reasoning and arguing. Indeed, there are several basic terms that need to be made clear to the reader.

Inference. When a person draws a conclusion from a body of information, he or she is inferring, or drawing an inference. Inferring is a mental act. (For example, I see thunderclouds approaching and infer that there will be a rainstorm soon.) Inferring is widely taken to be the paradigm of *reasoning.*

Implication. The two sentences, (1) "There are thunderclouds approaching" and (2) "There are clouds approaching" are logically related: (1) implies (2)—if (1) is true, then (2) must also be true. Implication relationships, such that if one sentence (set) is true, then another sentence must necessarily also be true, are the subject matter of classical formal logic. Implications are different from inferences: inference is a mental act, whereas implication is a relation among sentences or propositions. A person can recognize an implication without thereby drawing any inference; for example, if I already believe that thunderclouds are approaching, I do not also infer that there are clouds approaching, even if I recognize that the first implies the second. Logic is often said to consist of the rules of (valid) inference, but that is imprecise: logic really consists of the rules of (valid) implication relationships.

Argument. Argument has many different senses, but in any of them it is different from both inference and implication. In argument as evidence or proof, an argument is the reasons or evidence one has to support a belief or claim. Thus, for example, in theology there are arguments for the existence of a deity (for example, there must be a Prime Mover), and I think I have a good argument for buying a dog (we need the exercise and companionship, we love dogs, and we have the time and resources to care for a dog). In this sense of argument, we reason to (or infer) our point of view from reasons or evidence, and those reasons or evidence constitute the premises of our argument. Here there is a one-to-one correspondence between our inference and the resultant argument: the argument expresses or captures our reasoning.

In another sense of the term, arguments as tools of (rational) persuasion, an argument is discourse addressed to an audience (of one or more) with the intention of persuading the audience to accept a point of view. So lawyers address arguments to judges and juries, politicians argue against their opponents, and in journal articles scholars argue for the claims they advance. In this sense of argument the proponent invites the audience to draw an inference but need not draw that inference himself or herself. I might appeal to your Christian commitment to persuade you to donate money to a charitable cause, although because I am not a Christian myself that reason cannot be a reason that persuades me to give to that cause. In this sense an argument is an invitation to infer but is not, and does not necessarily express, an inference itself. Note, finally, that the relationship between the premises (reasons and evidence) and the conclusion of an argument in either sense may, but need not, be one of logical implication.

Is Good Nondeductive Reasoning Possible?

This last point is crucial. One of the key issues that informal logic works to address is whether the relationship between the premises and conclusions of good reasoning,[2] that is, cogent, rationally compelling reasoning, must be a logical implication. In other words, can there be good reasoning that is not logically valid—in which the truth of the premises does not necessitate the truth of the conclusion? The consensus among informal logicians is that there can be logically good, but nonvalid, reasoning. This is similarly an important question for evaluation practitioners and theorists, because the brunt of evaluative reasoning encountered in everyday practice is nondeductive.

One kind of example used to make the point is that there clearly can be good all-things-considered reasoning—reasoning in which there is a variety of reasons in favor of and against a particular viewpoint, but on balance (all things considered), the pros outweigh the cons (or vice versa). Most arguments for public policies have this feature, and, interestingly, this is the form of "putting things together" reasoning (House, this volume) or "synthesis" evaluations (Scriven, this volume) that is the fourth step in the "general logic" of evaluation (Fournier, this volume). Another example is reasoning from factual evidence to evaluative conclusions, which also must be possible if the practice of evaluation is to occur. There can be no relation of logical implication between the premises and conclusions of such reasoning—factual premises cannot necessitate evaluative conclusions—but it remains a problem how to explain the nature of and norms for such inferences. This is what Scriven calls the fundamental problem, for which he offers an explanation in his chapter in this volume. There is thus a central overlap between the concerns of informal logic and evaluation practitioners and theorists.

So if deductive implication is not the only measure of good reasoning, then what other kinds of good reasoning are there, and how else is reasoning or argument to be evaluated? Informal logicians have proposed various answers to these questions. To the extent that the reasoning used in the practice of evaluation is nondeductive, these solutions might prove fruitful in their application to evaluation practice.

Acceptability, Relevance, and Sufficiency Criteria. One proposal by informal logicians has been to evaluate reasoning in terms of the acceptability of the premises, their relevance, and their sufficiency or adequacy as support for the conclusion (Johnson and Blair, 1994b; Govier, 1992). Acceptability is relative to the purposes at hand and the practical constraints in place. Thus, although ideally one wants evidence known with certainty to be factual, in some contexts, when time and the cost of investigation are limited, the best one can get is what it is more or less reasonable to believe to be factual. Of course, in that case the conclusion must be qualified appropriately. Relevance has proven intractable to analysis (Woods, 1994), although the effort to explicate it is ongoing among informal logicians (see van Eemeren and Grootendorst, 1992; Tindale, 1994). A useful distinction has been made between global relevance—relevant from the broad perspective of the subject or topic in general—and local relevance—relevant in the particular component inference being drawn as one unit or aspect of the overall reasoning (Walton, 1989). Moreover, additional information can illuminate the relevance of data earlier thought to be irrelevant ("My client's left-handedness is relevant, your honor, because the defense will produce evidence that will prove that the murderer had to be right-handed!"). Sufficiency, like acceptability, will be a function of circumstances and needs. If a quick and dirty judgment is all that can be afforded by time and resources, the kinds, quality, and amount of evidence needed can be less than ideal, provided that the conclusions drawn are qualified accordingly.

Applied to evaluations, what counts as acceptable, relevant, and sufficient would in part seem to be a function of which game one is playing in making the evaluation (see Smith, this volume). Similarly, which criteria of evaluation and which weightings are relevant will be a function of the purposes of the activity or process being evaluated (see, for example, House's discussion of faculty evaluation, this volume). The importance assigned to variations between contexts in fact seems to be common to evaluation and informal logic, if the principal chapters of this volume are any indication. House's emphasis on the importance of adjusting criteria and weights to context is consistent with Smith's stressing the relevance of differences between societal games and with Fournier's insistence that working logics must vary to suit different approaches to evaluation. Informal logicians are increasingly sensitive to the relevance of the differences between kinds, purposes, and occasions of argument.

Informal Fallacies. Another way that has been proposed by informal logicians for the evaluation of arguments and reasoning is in terms of the presence or absence of informal fallacies. The scholarly analysis of informal fallacies has made enormous strides in quantity and quality in the past ten or fifteen years; their treatment even a decade ago has been largely superseded by much more sophisticated accounts (see Hansen's 1990 bibliography). It is increasingly agreed that many informal fallacies are patterns of otherwise good reasoning that have gone wrong, been misapplied, misused, or abused. Nowadays one speaks of good as well as bad ad hominem or slippery slope reasoning, just as one speaks of good or bad analogical reasoning. Moreover, many types or patterns of reasoning have been subjected to fine-grained analysis, so that, for example, several different kinds of ad hominem reasoning (abusive, circumstantial, tu quoque, and so on) or of analogical reasoning (inductive and a priori) have been distinguished, along with descriptions of a variety of ways each can go awry. Entire monographs have been devoted to single fallacies—that is, to one set of related patterns of sound reasoning and their associated miscues or misuses (for example, Walton, 1992).

A good example of a once-reviled argument pattern now rehabilitated is the argument from authority. At one time regarded as always fallacious, today arguing from authority is generally accepted as a sound, indeed practically necessary, basis of reasoning—provided that certain conditions are met. For instance, the claim based on authority must belong to a domain where expertise is applicable. For example, an appropriately qualified medical researcher can be cited to establish the developmental stages of the human fetus, but not its moral standing, which is a matter about which arguably there is no expertise that could justify accepting an opinion on someone's authority. The condition *appropriately qualified* is necessary because expertise is often narrow and highly specialized: for example, not all medical researchers are knowledgeable about fetal development. Also, should experts in a field disagree among themselves, the authoritativeness of the judgments of any one of them must be appropriately qualified. And so on. So ad verecundiam reasoning can be perfectly acceptable or it can be fallacious, depending on where and how it is used.

Fournier (this volume) has pointed out that the connoisseurial approach in evaluation entails a kind of appeal to expertise. Hence the discussions in the informal logic literature of the conditions for appropriate and inappropriate reliance on authority in reasoning might be applicable to this area of the practice of evaluation (for example, Johnson and Blair, 1994a; Govier, 1992; Walton, 1989). The use of fallacy analysis in the examination of evaluation proposals and reports might also be a useful tool for evaluators in identifying sound reasoning that supports resulting claims.

Argument Schemes. The analysis of the patterns of reasoning associated with traditional informal fallacies has been connected with a revival of the descriptive and normative analysis of argument schemes in general that has recently emerged in European circles studying argumentation (Schellens, 1987; van Eemeren and Kruiger, 1987; Kienpointner, 1987, 1992). There seems to be a finite number of patterns of reasoning in use, and only some subset of these are cogent, in the respect that actual reasoning following the pattern tends to yield defensible conclusions starting from plausible premises or data (for example, generalizing certain properties of a sample to a population in sampling or survey research, or the appeal to analogies between cases in arguments from precedent).

Clearly some argument schemes will be appropriate for some purposes, and others for other purposes. Some theorists have proposed that we formulate all the conditions for the good patterns of reasoning. Others have argued that, because these inferences are nondeductive, no finite decision procedure is possible, and so instead an understanding of each argument scheme should be used to generate an associated set of critical questions. Thus, for instance, for reasoning based on an appeal to expertise or authority, it is appropriate to raise such questions as, "Is there established knowledge in this field on this topic at this time?" and "Is there any reason, such as a conflict of interest, to distrust this expert's veracity or candor on this occasion?" Given that there are identifiable, frequently used patterns of reasoning deployed in generating and formulating evaluations of different sorts, this model of identifying the salient features of such patterns and formulating sets of associated critical questions (see Schellens, 1987) would seem to be applicable to how practitioners design, implement, and modify evaluations, ultimately strengthening every-day practice.

The Toulmin Model. Another approach to analyzing and evaluating reasoning that has come lately to informal logic is the use of the model of argument introduced by Toulmin (1958), presented in this volume in some detail by Fournier (see Freeman, 1991, for a contemporary informal logic adaptation). The Toulmin model has the great merit of sorting issues about what the evidence is from issues about what rules or principles or other generalizations justify drawing any conclusions from the evidence. Some informal logicians (for example, Blair, 1992; Freeman, 1992) have proposed that Toulmin's warrants function as relevance-screens, and by the same token they specify conditions of sufficiency as well.

Fournier (this volume) has pointed out that, and illustrated how, the Toulmin model works well to map the reasoning of the many component inferences contributing to any evaluation. Thus, using House's example in this volume, the warrant-supporting argument for research ability in faculty evaluation would be the criteria and standards for research developed for that faculty evaluation system, and the warrant for any particular judgment of research ability would be the application of those criteria and standards to the facts of a candidate's research record. I am skeptical, however, about the model's usefulness for illuminating the reasoning used at the synthesizing stage of evaluation. As House points out, there seems to be no set of metacriteria and standards for summing up the scores on the various disparate component elements into an overall evaluation. Mechanical weight-and-sum methods "lack subtlety and finesse," House says, and Scriven goes so far as to claim that most of them are invalid. So the prospects for a useful, general, synthesizing warrant are not yet promising.

Reasoning as Dialectical

Many informal logicians are coming to see argumentation as being in principle dialectical (and frequently so in practice, too). That is, an argument in the sense of reasons for a claim is seen as a move offered in an argument; an argument in the sense of an attempt to persuade an interlocutor is understood as part of an actual or possible exchange between parties who differ over the truth or merits of a particular viewpoint, each trying to convince the other. Our reasoning, so conceived, is not the private musings of isolated individuals. Instead, the reasons we produce to support a claim are best understood as designed to respond to particular doubts or questions about its truth or merits that others have raised or might raise (see van Eemeren and Grootendorst, 1984; Blair and Johnson, 1987; Freeman, 1991, gives a dialectical spin to Toulmin's model). Considered in this light, the requirement of sufficiency would include the need to meet all the objections that are known to have been leveled against the claim in question. And data or evidence would be acceptable only if it would pass unchallenged by people knowledgeable about such matters.

It might be that this dialectical perspective could serve a useful purpose in the practice of evaluation. For instance, it does seem to serve as a kind of check on the practitioner who is always faced with the lurking question, "Would this judgment stand up to the scrutiny of my peers?" and more specifically, "Does my use of this method get around the criticism leveled against such methods in the latest journal article on the point, and if not, can I defend it against that criticism?"

Practice Informing Theory

The theory related to the understanding of arguments and reasoning, their interpretation and their evaluation that has been developing in informal logic over the past 25 years has its roots in concrete practical questions. We began wanting to teach our students how to analyze and criticize arguments found in public discourse, with a view to getting a better understanding of the truth of the matter (to whatever extent it might be available). Students wanted to evaluate President Johnson's and Secretary McNamara's defense of the U.S. involvement in the Vietnam War (I was a graduate student at Michigan in the 1960s); they wanted to know whether a good case could be made for affirmative action; they wanted to reason their way to a position on abortion rights they could support. Working with the tool we had been taught in graduate school to use, formal logic, we found it cumbersome and often inapplicable or unenlightening. So we began to develop our own tools, which in turn led to an informal logic theory with increasing sophistication, which in turn illuminated the practice of reasoning and argumentation. The acid test has always been, and must be, how well it works when applied to actual reasoning, to the arguments found in use in public discourse. Theory arose out of practice and returns to inform practice.

My speculation is that the same kind of connection between practice and theory found in informal logic exists in the field of evaluation. Evaluation practitioners started with practical tasks and used the available social science theoretical models as best they could. In the process of tailoring these methodologies to apply to different kinds of evaluations, including increasingly complex ones, they found that they had to attend to the assumptions that their methods presupposed and subject them to critical scrutiny. Thus emerged greater self-consciousness about methodology and increasingly sophisticated revisions of earlier approaches, as well as the introduction of novel methods and approaches. At the heart of all this activity is the reasoning involved in drawing inferences from the information base plus the evaluative principles (criteria, standards, and so on) to the evaluative conclusions, in the generation of criteria and of information-gathering methods (warrant-establishing reasoning, for example), and in the formation of an overall evaluative conclusion based on the component evaluative judgments. In sum, the conscientious practice of evaluation must be attentive to its component reasoning practices and in the process develops improved methods that are tested back in the field, in terms of their usefulness to practitioners. But as with informal logic, the theorist and the practitioner are ideally one and the same person. The practitioner ignorant of theoretical developments does a poor job. Moreover, the theorist must be empirical. (This is another respect in which theory should be context sensitive.) A prioristic theories forced onto recalcitrant subject matter, like a wrong-sized shoe, produce only distorted analyses of arguments and reasoning, and I expect the same would be true for evaluations.

Informal Logic as a Subfield of Evaluation

That there might be connections between informal logic and evaluation is not surprising because, after all, informal logic is itself a branch of evaluation. Although evaluation practitioners focus on the objects of evaluation to which their daily work applies, such as products, programs, and personnel, and no contracts are tendered to evaluate arguments, evaluation as a field is in principle applicable to anything that might be evaluated. Movie reviews and literary criticism are species of evaluation, and so too is the critique of arguments and reasoning in general.

Applications of Evaluation to Informal Logic

From this point of view, the insights about its own reasoning developed in the field of professional evaluation are likely to transfer to informal logic. Thus Scriven's analysis of probative reasoning, developed in relation to evaluation, applies to reasoning in general and is of great interest to informal logicians. Similarly, the advice about synthesis reasoning that House offers is applicable to inferences wherever disparate and conflicting data must be somehow assimilated into a single, balanced, overall judgment. Smith's caution to attend to the game that is in play to determine what criteria and standards are relevant applies equally well to the evaluation of arguments, and it is mirrored in the distinctions in informal logic by Walton (1989) between different kinds of dialogue and his discussion of the dangers of applying the criteria appropriate to one type to another, or of shifting in mid-discussion from one type to another (for example, from a rational disagreement resolution-type dialogue to a quarrel-type dialogue). Fournier's distinction between general logic and working logic is parallel to the distinction in informal logic between general principles of argument evaluation (such as relevance, sufficiency, and acceptability) and the fine-grained analyses of individual informal fallacies.

Therefore, from the point of view of informal logic practice and theory there is common ground for conversation with evaluation theorists and practitioners. I look forward to a continued dialogue.

Notes

1. This is not the place for an extended discussion of the nature of informal logic and its defining problems. Readers interested in a series of overviews of the field at different points in its development should consult Johnson and Blair (1980, 1985, 1994a, 1994b).
2. To avoid cumbersomeness I will henceforth use *reasoning* when I mean to refer to reasoning or arguments, except to emphasize both or to indicate when the distinction makes a difference.

References

Blair, J. A., and Johnson, R. H. "Argumentation as Dialectical." *Argumentation,* 1987, *1* (1), 41-56.

Blair, J. A. "Premissary Relevance." *Argumentation,* 1992, *6* (2), 203-217.

Freeman, J. B. *Dialectics and the Macrostructure of Argument: A Theory of Argument Structure.* Amsterdam: Mouton de Gruyter, 1991.

Freeman, J. B. "Relevance, Warrants, Backing, Inductive Support." *Argumentation,* 1992, *6* (2), 219-235.

Govier, T. *A Practical Study of Argument.* (3rd ed.). Belmont, Calif.: Wadsworth, 1992.

Hansen, H. V. "An Informal Logic Bibliography." *Informal Logic,* 1990, *3,* 155-184.

Johnson, R. H., and Blair, J. A. "The Recent Development of Informal Logic." In J. A. Blair and R. H. Johnson (eds.), *Informal Logic, The First International Symposium.* Inverness, Calif.: Edgepress, 1980.

Johnson, R. H., and Blair, J. A. "Informal Logic, the Past Five Years, 1987–1993." *American Philosophical Quarterly,* 1985, *22,* 181-196.

Johnson, R. H., and Blair, J. A. *Logical Self-Defense.* New York: McGraw-Hill, 1994a.

Johnson, R. H., and Blair, J. A. "Informal Logic, Past and Present." In R. H. Johnson and J. A. Blair (eds.), *New Essays in Informal Logic.* Windsor, Ontario: Informal Logic, 1994b.

Kienpointner, M. "Towards a Typology of Argument Schemes." In F. H. van Eemeren, R. Grootendorst, J. A. Blair, and C. A. Willard (eds.), *Argumentation: Across the Lines of Discipline. Proceedings of the Conference on Argumentation 1986, 3.* Dordrecht, The Netherlands: Foris, 1987.

Kienpointner, M. *Alltagslogik, Struktur und Funktion von Argumentationsmustern.* Stuttgart: Fromann-Holzboog, 1992.

Schellens, P. J. "Types of Argument and the Critical Reader." In F. H. van Eemeren, R. Grootendorst, J. A. Blair, and C. A. Willard (eds.), *Argumentation: Analyses and Practices. Proceedings of the Conference on Argumentation 1986, 3B.* Dordrecht, The Netherlands: Foris, 1987.

Tindale, C. W. "Contextual Relevance in Argumentation." In R. H. Johnson and J. A. Blair (eds.), *New Essays in Informal Logic.* Windsor, Ontario: Informal Logic, 1994.

Toulmin, S. *The Uses of Argument.* Cambridge, Mass.: Cambridge University Press, 1958.

van Eemeren, F. H., and Grootendorst, R. *Speech Acts in Argumentative Discourse: A Theoretical Model for the Analysis of Discussions Directed Towards Solving Conflicts of Opinion.* New York: De Gruyter, 1984.

van Eemeren, F. H., and Kruiger, T. "Identifying Argumentation Schemes." In F. H. van Eemeren, R. Grootendorst, J. A. Blair, and C. A. Willard (eds.), *Argumentation: Across the*

Lines of Discipline. Proceedings of the Conference on Argumentation 1986, 3A. Dordrecht, The Netherlands: Foris, 1987, 70-81.

van Eemeren, F. H., and Grootendorst, R. (eds.). Special issue on relevance. *Argumentation*, 1992, 6 (2).

Walton, D. *Informal Logic: A Handbook for Critical Argumentation*. Cambridge, Mass.: Cambridge University Press, 1989.

Walton, D. *Begging the Question: Circular Reasoning as a Tactic of Argumentation*. New York: Greenwood Press, 1991.

Walton, D. *Slippery Slope Arguments*. Oxford: Clarendon Press, 1992.

Woods, J. "Sunny Prospects for Relevance?" In R. H. Johnson and J. A. Blair (eds.), *New Essays in Informal Logic*. Windsor, Ontario: Informal Logic, 1994.

J. ANTHONY BLAIR *is professor of philosophy at the University of Windsor, Ontario, Canada, and coeditor of the journal* Informal Logic.

Perceptual control theory of human behavior suggests to evaluators how to reach warranted syntheses legitimately even though their judgments are inevitably dependent on context and the purposes of the stakeholders.

Purpose, Context, and Synthesis: Can We Avoid Relativism?

Hugh G. Petrie

This volume is particularly welcome in this day and age. It appears in a context of postmodernism, deconstructionism, and poststructuralism, at a time when we are confronted with a plethora of claims concerning different ways of knowing, within a milieu in which the most important issue seems to be whether or not everyone's voice is heard. It sometimes seems as if reasoning, justification, validity, evidence, and claims of better and worse are relics of a bygone age. From individual relationships to talk shows to politics, everyone's opinion appears to be as good as everyone else's on almost any matter whatsoever. The very ideas of evaluation and the logic of evaluation would seem to be suspect. Truth and goodness seem to many to be relative to one's race, class, gender, and point of view.

However, the issue is not so simple as rejecting the relativists and returning to the good old days of revealed truth and positivistic science. Several of the most influential scholars in evaluation, including those in this volume, have been among the leaders in showing the limitations of classical, absolutist theories of truth, reasoning, and evaluation. They have expounded on the extent to which evaluation is relative to the purposes of the stakeholders, is context dependent, can yield different results using different kinds of evaluation, and is different within different ways of knowing. These are precisely the kinds of results pounced on by the relativists as undermining the possibility of using reasoning to reach warranted evaluative conclusions. Yet I believe that the authors remain committed to the legitimacy of evaluative reasoning.

So the present volume comes at a critical time as it tries to steer a course between the Scylla of absolutism and the Charybdis of relativism. What kinds of logic and reasoning might allow us to make warranted evaluative judgments, at least of better and worse, but that nonetheless appear to require the following features?

- The judgments are dependent on the purposes, both individual and social, of the evaluator.
- The judgments are also dependent on the context in which the evaluation takes place; that is, the context determines the judgments that actually occur.
- Despite not being able to prespecify all of the evaluative criteria and how they will play out in a given context, we can make warranted evaluative syntheses, all things considered.

These three themes—purpose, context, and synthesis—pervade to a greater or lesser extent each of the four chapters. These themes are fundamental to a proper understanding of reasoning in evaluation, and each of the authors explores how a properly understood logic of evaluation can take them into account.

In the end, however, it appears that the authors share with the relativists a conception of context-dependent purposive human behavior that allows relativism to be seen as a plausible alternative. I will, therefore, add to their contributions by suggesting that the perceptual control theory view of human behavior gives an account of the interaction of purpose and context that renders warranted evaluative reasoning entirely plausible.

Purpose

The major contribution of the four main chapters is that, together, they implicitly show how at least some purposes can enter into evaluative reasoning in a perfectly straightforward, nonrelativistic way. Utilizing the notions of criterial definition and probative inference, Scriven demonstrates that many of the key concepts about which we wish to reason evaluatively have, as part of their criterial definitions, evaluative features. Then by making use of some very general, noncontroversial notions of merit we can infer to evaluative conclusions from the definitions of the items of interest along with certain factual premises. For example, if we know that the purpose of a cooking pot is to hold liquid, we can conclude that a leaky pot will not be nearly as good as one that does not leak.

However, purpose need not be considered as an essential part of the definition of a concept only in such "functional" cases. It also is part of the concepts of more overtly value-laden activities as well. As Smith describes in the evaluation of the *Iowa* explosion, the conclusion we reach will depend on whether we start with the concept of a legal liability to be adjudicated or a social scientific question to be resolved. The former concept relies heavily on expert opinion, whereas the latter is defined by generalizability and replicability. Thus Smith takes us beyond the individual purposes of clients, evaluators, and stakeholders to examine the societal purposes built into different games we have chosen to play in our social lives. He reminds us that human beings create certain kinds of social structures to carry out fundamental purposes shared across large groups of people, and as such those purposes serve as evaluative criteria within the concepts of these structures.

Fournier elaborates the discussion of purpose with her useful distinction between general and working logics. The purpose of general logic is to identify criteria, construct standards, devise measurements, and synthesize judgments. The purpose of a given working logic is to begin to flesh out these general features with the specific criteria, say, of a causal approach to the evaluation of program interventions. It would not be too much of a stretch to suggest that Fournier's working logic notion is a theoretical elaboration of Smith's ideas of societal games. As she describes the notion of working logic, in a connoisseurial approach to evaluation, for example, we would know from the concept of a connoisseur that legitimate evaluative conclusions from that approach will reflect the way it feels to an expert to be involved in the program.

House gives an extended example of the societal game of professors in a research university judging their colleagues for promotion and tenure. The purpose of such a game is to maintain the scholarly capacities of the university, and its working logic is expressed in the preparation of dossiers, letters from external referees, promotion and tenure committees, and the like.

The point is that the concepts we have, both of functional things and of social activities, carry a number of evaluative criteria within their very definitions. If we understand the concepts, then along with our experience in actually using those concepts to deal with the world we can, and often do, straightforwardly come to warranted evaluative conclusions. If we want to buy a cooking pot or a car, we compare what we see with the purposes of the pot or car and act accordingly. If we understand the purpose of the research university, we compare a candidate's dossier with our concept of a full professor and vote our conscience. If our purpose is to improve inner-city education, we compare a program's effects with our ideal of inner-city education and act accordingly. There simply is no logical gap between understanding a concept and being able to make evaluative judgments about instances of that concept in the real world in which we live our lives.

This is, of course, not to say that our concepts are immutable. In light of experience and other, higher-order goals, we can change and modify our concepts. With the advent of microwave cookery, certain metallic materials are no longer desirable in a cooking pot. As the social contract between society and the university is renegotiated more in the direction of undergraduate teaching and service, the concept of the full professor changes as well, as House notes in his chapter. Our concept of health care has gradually been evolving toward one that includes consideration for the quality of life as well as for its mere length. The process of reaching warranted judgments, however, remains the same. We compare our experience in the particular context with the evaluative criteria contained in the concept and the judgments follow.

Purpose and Context

Typically, we view context as affecting the results of an evaluation when, roughly speaking, the same products or programs are being evaluated in different contexts with, perhaps, different results. For example, a Head Start program that works in one context is a disaster in another. In such a situation, we may well ask whether we can reach a warranted evaluation of whether Head Start is a good program or not. Indeed, this recurring phenomenon is the bane of much program evaluation.

Smith's example, on the other hand, emphasizes the fact that not only can the same societal game be played in different contexts, but sometimes different societal games with different purposes played in the same context can give different results. Fournier's notion of working logics likewise accents ways in which different purposes compel us to deal with different parts of the context. The working logics begin to fill in the major outlines of what features of the context will be relevant in any given evaluation such as causal, connoisseurial, and the like. In short, context and purpose are inextricably intertwined.

However, whether it is the same game played in different contexts or different games played in the same context, the key point is that what counts as contextually relevant is dependent on the purposes and goals of the evaluator, the other stakeholders, and the evaluation game being played. In the absence of these purposes, context is just another name for everything that there is—a notion much too all-encompassing to be of any use. Thus the fact that a given professor is a good spouse and parent is, for the most part, irrelevant to the promotion game, although it may be quite relevant to the good colleague and friend game. Furthermore, the candidate's friendships in the third grade are likely irrelevant to both (although if the candidate married a third-grade friend it could become relevant to the good colleague and friend game).

This last example illustrates an important feature of the ways in which purposes actually determine contexts. We tend to think that if we know the purposes of a given evaluation, we can derive criteria that will prespecify what parts of the context will be relevant, and, of course, to some extent, that is possible. However, as the examples of the four authors so abundantly demonstrate, whenever one thinks one has taken all of the contextual features into account, one can always construct a plausible story as to why something we forgot to consider is relevant after all.

This is an important theoretical point. Purposes do not determine contextually relevant features in a top-down way. Rather it is because of our ability to experience the world in light of our purposes that we find out what parts of the context are relevant. Actually performing the evaluation, gathering data, forming judgments, and considering alternative scenarios in the concrete setting of the evaluation all are compared to the desired purposes to determine the extent to which any of these activities actually seems to be contributing to the evaluation.

In this regard, House's claim that context limits possibilities seems to be exactly right. He illustrates this in numerous ways in discussing faculty evaluation. He comments on how letters of reference are important, but less so if from former advisors; how research is important, but a Nobel prize winner's research may outweigh all sorts of other criteria; and so on. The purposes do not preselect the relevant context; rather, the particular context triggers criteria in terms of which we are experiencing the situation.

Warranted Syntheses

The central question of House's chapter is how a synthesis of various evaluations can be put together to reach a warranted evaluative judgment. He suggests that one often can, and, indeed, must put together the most coherent account possible of an evaluation. For House, coherence is the mark of a warranted synthesis. However, he emphasizes that the coherence depends on data and evidence and is always context bound. It is a coherent synthesis for the particular case and may or may not generalize easily, or at all, to other cases. His concrete examples are persuasive. The evaluative descriptions of the syntheses seem to make sense, at least to most people. Nevertheless, the evaluative logic of the coherence criterion for House remains elusive. As he says, we can more often attain it than we can analyze it.

The other authors also give numerous examples of plausible syntheses of various evaluations being reached. But examples are not a theory of evaluative reasoning. If, as the authors seem to believe, evaluative judgments are relative to purposes, individual and social, how can we reach a warranted synthesis? If evaluative judgments are relative to context and it is not possible to pre-specify the criteria that are relevant in the context, this is not just a complete capitulation to relativism? Despite the authors' examples, we still do not have any kind of account of how it is possible to account for purpose and context without falling into a radical relativism that simply says, "That's your story and I have mine."

It would be logically possible to try to address the threat of such a radical relativism by considering alternative conceptions of logic, or different "ways of knowing," or similar stratagems that might alleviate the tension between allowing for the relevance of purpose and context, and synthesis and the desire to reach warranted evaluative syntheses. There is, however, another alternative. The problem may lie not with our traditional conceptions of logic but with our traditional conceptions of human action that seem to treat purpose as at best a convenient fiction and at worst a mystifying superstition regarding human activity. It may be that with a more adequate conception of purposive human action, the threat of radical relativism will dissipate without the invention of new, esoteric logics or ways of knowing.

Perceptual Control Theory

Interestingly, over the past twenty years or so, a small, still largely unknown, body of work has begun to emerge that promises to meet the challenges to the logic of evaluation posed by the fact that our evaluative judgments are relative to our purposes, and the fact that the context determines the judgments that occur. This conception of human behavior was given its most powerful formulation by W. T. Powers (1973) in his book *Behavior: The Control of Perception*. Most recently in education, it has been the subject of a spirited debate in the pages of *Educational Researcher* (Cziko, 1992a, 1992b; Amundson, Serlin, and Lehrer, 1992). Researchers from a variety of other disciplines are also contributing to this body of research in general psychology (Powers, 1989, 1992; Robertson and Powers, 1990), experimental psychology (Bourbon, 1990; Hershberger, 1988; Marken, 1986, 1989, 1990, 1992), clinical psychology (Ford, 1989, 1994; Goldstein, 1990), education (Bohannon, Powers, and Schoepfle, 1974; Petrie, 1974, 1979, 1981, 1986), sociology (McClelland, 1994; McPhail, 1991; McPhail, Powers, and Tucker, 1992), ethology (Plooij, 1984; Plooij and van deRijt-Plooij, 1990), law (Gibbons, 1990), management (Forssell, 1993), and economics (Williams, 1989, 1990).

This new conception of human nature is called perceptual control theory, and as the title of Powers' book implies, it fundamentally turns our conception of human action on its head. Instead of viewing behavior as the outcome of stimuli or perceptions (as modified by cognition, emotions, or planning), perceptual control theory views behavior as the means by which a perceived state of affairs is brought to and maintained at a (frequently varying) reference or goal state.

Perceptual control theory makes use of the idea of the "circular causation" found in engineering control and servomechanism theory. Thermostats and cruise control systems are everyday examples of mechanical control systems that keep the perception of temperature or speed near the reference levels set for them. Such physical control systems were invented precisely because engineers wanted to create mechanical systems that behaved as we humans do as we go about the tasks of governing temperature, maintaining speed, tracking targets, and, in general, successfully pursuing our goals in a constantly changing environment. In doing so they created a theory that is much more amenable to modeling actual human behavior than the stimulus-response, input-output, independent variable-dependent variable kind of theory created by the psychologists.

How does perceptual control theory meet the challenges to evaluative logic outlined above? This brief space does not allow a full accounting of the theory, but perhaps I can draw enough analogies with familiar mechanical control systems to pique the interest of the reader in this revolutionary approach to understanding human behavior.

I will start with purpose. A central function of perceptual control theory is to account for intentionality and purpose. The fundamental phenomenon of human action is that we constantly are able to achieve our purposes or ends with varying means in a continuously changing environment. Control systems are precisely what allows that to occur.

Consider the mechanical cruise control system. There are an indefinite number of factors that might keep a car from maintaining a certain speed: headwinds, crosswinds, hills, curves, poor-quality gasoline, and so on. If we tried to build a mechanical system that would be able to determine how any of these features might interfere with the desired speed (which itself might change from time to time during a trip) and also include the capacity for calculating just how much gas to deliver to the engine to overcome any of these disturbances, we might well conclude that we could not possibly build a cruise control system.

Similarly, if we try to specify our evaluation criteria completely before the fact and give appropriate weights to the various criteria for a good professor before we enter into the actual evaluation, we might well conclude that a completely warranted evaluation is not possible either. As House illustrates, we cannot possibly anticipate every nuance of context that might make a difference.

But the engineers did not try to anticipate every potential disturbance to maintaining speed. Rather, they built a mechanism that sensed the speed of the car, compared that speed to the desired one, and, if it was too slow, fed more gas to the engine and, if too fast, decreased the gas. The cruise control neither knows nor cares what factors in the environment cause the speed to depart from its desired level; it just compensates when it does. In short, it controls the perception of the speed of the car, keeping it very close to the desired level, and it does this in a circular causation kind of way in which the output affects the input at the same time as the input is being compared with the reference speed and the difference between the two is actuating the output.

Note, too, that this is just how the human driver without cruise control behaves. We do not check headwinds or hills, especially if they are slight, and compute how much to depress or let up on the accelerator. Rather we monitor the speedometer and no matter what the cause of a change in the speed we want to maintain, we depress or let up on the accelerator accordingly.

Similarly, the human evaluator monitors the situation in light of the evaluation criteria contained in the concept of what is being evaluated. The evaluator gathers data, learns about the stakeholders, considers alternative scenarios in the concrete setting of the evaluation, and uses whatever information comes from the actual case to form the appropriate evaluative judgment.

Context is simply the world that we experience. A part of the world becomes important to us if it constitutes a disturbance to some part of the experience we are trying to control. We recognize the disturbance as a difference in what we perceive compared to what we want to perceive, and in a well-functioning control system our actions tend to move our perceptions in the directions we want to see. Control systems do not need to have a prespecification of the context in which they operate; they only need to be able to sense changes in the perceptual variables they are trying to control, whatever causes those changes. It is through conceiving purposeful action as the operation of a control system, controlling for seeing the world as its purpose defines it, that we understand how purpose defines the context but cannot predetermine what will be relevant.

Context limits the possibilities. Within the range of those features of the context that might actually affect the evaluation, through collecting data, sifting evidence, and generally becoming familiar with the particular case, the evaluator senses those features that affect the overall goal of judging how well the product or process or program comes up to the concept of that product, process, or program. Because, as Scriven has shown, the evaluative criteria are, at least in part, built into the concept of what is being evaluated, comparing the actual situation to that concept automatically results in a judgment of how closely the situation matches the concept. It really is true that there are a number of concepts that we may not be able to define, but that we can recognize when we see. We do not need to account for the Nobel Prize winner in setting forth criteria for promotion, but if we see one, we recognize the achievement as relevant.

In an evaluation, we have some concept of what the ideal cooking pot or professor or program should look like. We go about the job of examining a particular example of that cooking pot or professor or program and, to the extent that what we see, wherever it comes from, is different from what we want to see, we are able to issue evaluative judgments. Then, given our typical beliefs about the way the world of policy and evaluations work, we hope our judgments will lead to changes in our perceptions of how the pots, professors, and programs are dealt with, changed, modified, or judged by others. (Of course, sometimes our evaluative judgments do not lead to the results we would like, causing a disturbance to another of our goals as evaluators and leading to other activities, such as writing papers about the relationship of evaluation to policy. But that is another story that could also be accounted for by perceptual control theory.)

But someone may well object that other stories are precisely what distinguish real evaluations from mechanical cruise control systems. It may be interesting to note that the cruise control system does not have to prespecify the road conditions or weather or gasoline quality to maintain its set speed, but the real analogy to evaluation would lie in looking at situations in which it may be inappropriate to maintain the set speed at all. The cruise control system cannot help us there. It blindly maintains its set speed, even if, say, slowing and thickening traffic conditions call for a different speed. And, of course, this is correct. Analogies with mechanical control systems can go only so far, especially because most of the familiar ones are simple one-level control systems.

But consider the control system that is the human driver. The human driver is presumably maintaining the set speed in order to get somewhere. However, the driver presumably wants to get there safely as well, and all sorts of conditions may occur that would render a set speed inappropriate: traffic may slow; the speed limit may change; there may be an accident; a bridge may be flooded out; or the road may be slick from rain. There is no possible way that the human driver could prespecify all of the ways in which the trip at a given speed might become unsafe, but there is equally no question that when any of these things occur, we recognize them as a threat to our safe passage and change the speed accordingly.

We do some things in order to do others and those in order to pursue still higher-order purposes. The adaptable, intelligent person does not persist in behavior that does not serve higher-order goals but varies that behavior in an unpredictable, complex, and changing world in order to see the world as those higher-order goals specify it.

Perceptual control theory postulates the notion of a hierarchically arranged network of control systems such that the output of some of the higher levels changes the goals of the lower levels, bringing the whole into an equilibrium. This is what happens when we change the set speed of the cruise control in light of wanting to perceive ourselves as not crashing into the traffic ahead of us.

It is also in this way that we can begin to understand the idea of a coherent evaluative synthesis, even if we cannot prespecify how it would work out in particular cases. Consider House's promotion committee. Experienced professors have a concept of being a good professor in a research university without at all being able to define that concept in concrete terms. They sense the evidence regarding a given professor and can tell whether or not there is a deviation from their concept. Someone who receives poor undergraduate student ratings for teaching but has a record of successfully advising doctoral students can be seen as a good teacher of a different kind. An engineering professor who publishes few traditional journal articles but who is asked to serve on a national commission to set the standards for making concrete pipes is seen to be a good professor, exemplifying outstanding scholarship in a nontraditional way.

Our concept of a good professor plays the role of the desire to arrive where we are going safely in the driving example. Traditional refereed journal articles play a role analogous to the set speed in the cruise control system. We can recognize various ways in which refereed articles may contribute to research productivity, from top journals to prize-winning essays, without prespecifying all of these variations. At the same time, we can also see how maintaining an emphasis simply on refereed articles at all costs may lead us to a "traffic accident" with a professor who manifests outstanding research through an important consultative arrangement. We do not need to know all of the ways in which the context might affect our perception of the speed or the professor, but by comparing what we sense to our reference concepts, we know whether or not they fall short.

As House points out, we can even change our notion of a good professor in a research university as society presses us for better undergraduate teaching and more relevant research. The higher-order goal of those of us in the university maintaining a productive social contract with those who support us can vary the nature of lower-order goals we may have.

In an extremely important way, human beings are even more predictable than are physical events. Human beings are organized to attain consistent goals despite varying circumstances. An automobile mechanically programmed to drive around a given track will be less predictable in its path in the face of significant crosswinds than will the path of that same automobile in the hands of a human driver wanting to drive around the track. An evaluator applying predetermined criteria of evaluation will be less likely to reach a warranted synthesis than one alert to the unpredictable nuances of the actual case.

Thus there is nothing deficient in a logic of evaluation that does not allow us to specify in advance all the evaluative criteria and how different contexts might be judged in light of those criteria. Indeed, that is just what human beings, conceived as behaving so as to control their perceptions, do all the time. It is the only way in which we can make sense of the human capacity to achieve consistent results in a constantly changing environment.

We need not fear for the validity of evaluative syntheses that recognize the relativity to the purpose of the evaluation and to the context. By sensing the various nuances of the context, we are in effect comparing the actual context with our concept of that which we are evaluating. Because control systems control perceptions, not behavior, we need not know in advance what the details of the context might be. Once we have compared the concrete situation to our concept, however, we can describe the extent to which the situation meets or fails to meet our concept. In short, we can legitimately make warranted evaluative judgments.

References

Amundson, R., Serlin, R. C., and Lehrer, R. "On the Threats That Do *Not* Face Educational Research." *Educational Researcher,* 1992, *21* (9), 19–24.

Bohannon, P., Powers, W. T., and Schoepfle, M. "Systems Conflict in the Learning Alliance." In L. J. Stiles (ed.), *Theories for Teaching.* New York: Dodd, Mead, 1974.

Bourbon, W. T. "Invitation to the Dance: Explaining the Variance When Control Systems Interact." *American Behavioral Scientist,* 1990, *34* (1), 95–105.

Cziko, G. A. "Perceptual Control Theory: One Threat to Educational Research Not (Yet?) Faced by Amundson, Serlin, and Lehrer." *Educational Researcher,* 1992a, *21* (9), 25–27.

Cziko, G. A. "Purposeful Behavior as the Control of Perception: Implications for Educational Research." *Educational Researcher,* 1992b, *21* (9), 10–18.

Ford, E. E. *Freedom from Stress.* Scottsdale, Ariz.: Brandt, 1989.

Ford, E. E. *Discipline for Home and School.* Scottsdale, Ariz.: Brandt, 1994.

Forssell, D. C. "Perceptual Control: A New Management Insight." *Engineering Management Journal,* 1993, *5* (4), 1–7.

Gibbons, H. *The Death of Jeffrey Stapleton: Exploring the Way Lawyers Think.* Concord, N.H.: Franklin Pierce Law Center, 1990.

Goldstein, D. M. "Clinical Applications of Control Theory." *American Behavioral Scientist,* 1990, *34* (1), 110–116.

Hershberger, W. A. (ed.). *Volitional Action: Conation and Control.* Amsterdam: Elsevier, 1988.

McClelland, K. "Perceptual Control and Social Power." *Sociological Perspectives,* 1994, *37,* 461–496.

McPhail, C. *The Myth of the Madding Crowd.* New York: Aldine DeGruyter, 1991.

McPhail, C., Powers, W. T., and Tucker, C. W. "Simulating Individual and Collective Action in Temporary Gatherings." *Social Science Computer Review,* 1992, *10* (1), 1–28.

Marken, R. S. "Perceptual Organization of Behavior: A Hierarchical Control Model of Coordinated Action." *Journal of Experimental Psychology: Human Perception and Performance,* 1986, *12,* 267–276.

Marken, R. S. "Behavior in the First Degree." In W. A. Hershberger (ed.), *Volitional Action: Conation and Control.* Amsterdam: Elsevier, 1989.

Marken, R. S. "Purposeful Behavior: The Control Theory Approach." *American Behavioral Scientist,* 1990, *34* (1), 6–13.

Marken, R. S. *Mindreadings: Experimental Studies of Purpose.* Gravel Switch, Ky.: CSG Books, 1992.

Petrie, H. G. "Action, Perception, and Education." *Educational Theory,* 1974, *24,* 33–45.

Petrie, H. G. "Against 'Objective' Tests: A Note on the Epistemology Underlying Current Testing Dogma." In M. N. Ozer (ed.), *A Cybernetic Approach to the Assessment of Children: Toward a More Humane Use of Human Beings.* Boulder, Colo.: Westview Press, 1979.

Petrie, H. G. *The Dilemma of Inquiry and Learning.* Chicago: University of Chicago Press, 1981.

Petrie, H. G. "Testing for Critical Thinking." *Proceedings of the Philosophy of Education Society 1985,* 1986.

Plooij, F. X. *The Behavioral Development of Free-Living Chimpanzee Babies and Infants.* Norwood, N.J.: Ablex, 1984.

Plooij, F. X., and van deRijt-Plooij, H. H. "Developmental Transitions as Successive Reorganizations of a Control Hierarchy." *American Behavioral Scientist,* 1990, *34* (1), 67–80.

Powers, W. T. *Behavior: The Control of Perception.* Hawthorne, N.Y.: Aldine DeGruyter, 1973.

Powers, W. T. *Living Control Systems: Selected Papers.* Gravel Switch, Ky.: CSG Books, 1989.

Powers, W. T. *Living Control Systems II: Selected Papers.* Gravel Switch, Ky.: CSG Books, 1992.

Robertson, R. J., and Powers, W. T. (eds.). *Introduction to Modern Psychology: The Control Theory View.* Gravel Switch, Ky.: CSG Books, 1990.

Williams, W. D. "Making It Clearer." *Continuing the Conversation: A Newsletter of Ideas in Cybernetics,* 1989, *18,* 9–10.

Williams, W. D. "The Giffen Effect: A Note on Economic Purposes." *American Behavioral Scientist,* 1990, *34* (1), 106–109.

HUGH G. PETRIE is professor of education and dean of the Graduate School of Education, State University of New York, Buffalo.

The reasoning process should be salient to the evaluator throughout the course of an evaluation.

Reasoning in Evaluation: Challenges for the Practitioner

Debra J. Rog

My response to the previous four chapters is shaped from the perspective of an evaluation practitioner who has given thought to theory and reasoning in the practice of evaluation. Although the vast majority of my experience has been with one approach to evaluation, program evaluation, I have had the opportunity to practice evaluation from several different venues: the federal government, a state legislative oversight agency, a private research firm, and a university-affiliated research institute. Therefore my perspective is colored by these different experiences in these venues, a number of which are discussed in this chapter.

Why Reasoning Should Be Important to the Evaluation Practitioner

What is expected as the bottom-line result of an evaluation should be considered at the top of an evaluation study. Evaluators begin by considering why the evaluation is being done in the first place. What is its purpose? What questions is it intended to answer? What are the information needs of the client and the stakeholders? Are there specific decisions that the evaluation can inform?

To reach a bottom line (or lines, as discussed later), there has to be a clear reasoning process not only when it is time to analyze and synthesize results but throughout the evaluation. How we draw evaluative conclusions is based on the underlying design of a study, the implementation of the methods, and the analysis and interpretation of the data collected. To make certain that the evidentiary base is of high quality and responsive to the question, and that claims can be made on the basis of this evidentiary base, the reasoning process

NEW DIRECTIONS FOR EVALUATION, no. 68, Winter 1995 © Jossey-Bass Publishers must be salient at all stages of the evaluation. As Fournier notes in this volume, the working logic of evaluation basically is the pattern of reasoning that builds defensible arguments.

In Hedrick, Bickman, and Rog (1993), we spoke of the trade-offs that inevitably face researchers in the design of a project. Based on limitations in dollar and staff resources, staff skills, time, and quality of available data, researchers often need to make trade-offs in the design of a study (such as how much of the resources should be spent on conducting interviews versus analyzing existing data sets). These trade-offs are best made with the ultimate conclusions in mind. In particular, we outlined three criteria for assessing these design trade-offs:

- *Credibility:* whether the design will be sufficiently sound to support the development of strong conclusions
- *Usefulness:* whether the decisions made continue to allow the design to be focused on the specific questions of interest
- *Feasibility:* whether the study is doable within the time and resource constraints

These same criteria are important to apply in the actual conduct of the evaluation. Even the best designs typically have to be modified in their implementation, particularly in areas where the programs and the phenomena are highly dynamic. For example, some evaluations are designed based on the expectation that there is a sufficient number of individuals in the "pipeline" to have the desired sample size for the treatment and control groups. However, if the number in the eligible pool of program participants is lower than expected, the design may need to be modified. The time frame for accepting people into the study may need to be lengthened, the eligibility criteria may need to be broadened, or some other change may be warranted. Whatever change is made should be made with a clear sense of how the ultimate conclusions will be affected. For example, broadening the eligibility criteria will change the population focus of the study and in turn the applicability of the study findings. If a change is not made, the sample size will be lowered and the ability of the study to detect expected effects will be weakened. Therefore understanding the reasoning process is critical if we are to make judgments throughout an evaluation that continue to lead us in the direction of drawing relevant, useful, and sound conclusions.

Reasoning in Practice: Six Challenges

From my review of the four previous chapters, six issues related to the reasoning process emerged that present challenges to the practitioner:

- Clarifying the evaluator role one is willing to play
- Evaluating fuzzy phenomena
- Getting to the bottom line

- Presenting the bottom line
- Providing internal explanation
- Deciding whether to offer recommendations.

Clarifying the Evaluator Role. In Chapter One Smith provides an important illustration of how the broader context can influence the evaluative strategy. He contends that it is the goals of the societal game (such as the social reform game or the social science game) in which an evaluator is involved that influences what problems are addressed, which phenomena are studied, and what outcomes are sought. Smith suggests that the debates in evaluation are focused not so much on what evaluative strategies are best in a given game but which game the evaluators ought to be playing.

I believe Smith has identified a useful way to frame the debate that has been gripping the evaluation profession. Unfortunately, the lack of agreement among those who practice evaluation on the games that are appropriate for evaluators has had the effect of confusing evaluation sponsors and others on the periphery of the profession. The most confusion has come from what Smith has termed "informal games" of social movements and special interests. What a stakeholder expects from an evaluation can be influenced by the roles or games that they have watched other evaluators play. For example, although it may be clear to all involved that the evaluator's formal game is social science, there may be less clarity as to whether they would be involved in social reform, particularly at the stage at which the results are presented and communicated. Therefore, in practice, it may be necessary to clarify at the outset to oneself and the client the games one is willing to play and not willing to play, and to reinforce this position at various points in the evaluation.

Evaluating Fuzzy Phenomena. A theme across the chapters is the importance of the phenomenon and nature of the phenomenon in the logic of evaluation. Both Scriven and Fournier emphasize the importance of a full understanding of the phenomenon to the logic of evaluation. As Fournier explicates, drawing on Scriven's work, without a deep-seated understanding of the phenomenon, the criteria selected to measure and evaluate the phenomenon may be faulty.

In emergent problem areas (Edwards, 1987), however, the nature of the phenomenon, such as homelessness, is often not well understood before action is taken. Ill-defined interventions are implemented in which there is a lack of explicit theoretical or conceptual framework as well as an absence of a well-developed understanding of the program (Rog, 1994). These interventions often are conducted when the political, social, and human pressures for action are great and the problem so severe as to warrant immediate action such that there is not the luxury of time to develop a sufficient knowledge base on the problem or an elegant, well-thought-out strategy for intervention. Homelessness in the 1980s was one of these emerging problem areas. Demonstration initiatives and other ameliorative strategies were sponsored while more basic research on the problem (studies of the size and characteristics of the population, for example) was being conducted.

For ill-defined interventions, I have described an expanded role for program evaluation. One area of expansion is to place more emphasis on understanding the phenomenon itself.

In an ongoing evaluation of a nine-city study of homeless families, begun in August 1990 (see Rog, 1991, for a description of this effort), the decision was made to collect fairly extensive descriptive data on the families participating in the initiative. Among the questions posed were the following: what does family homelessness look like across the nine cities? Why do families become homeless? What have been their histories of stability? Although part of the purpose of this expanded data collection was to provide a basis for assessing the implementation of the program eligibility criteria in the selection of families and the comparability of the families across sites, another reason for collecting an extensive amount of descriptive data was to expand knowledge of the phenomenon for future interventions.

Getting to the Bottom Line(s). One of the most difficult areas in evaluation is arriving at a bottom line. As House addresses, it is now standard practice within evaluation to examine multiple stakeholder interests, goals, processes, and outcomes with multiple methods and data sources. We look for convergence and triangulation within our data and strive for the most coherent explanations, even in the face of some conflicts. However, this is often easier said in theory than done in practice. Both House and Scriven acknowledge the difficulties in weighing evidence and offer a few strategies for synthesizing the data.

In reviewing the chapters by House and Scriven, I was reminded of some practical challenges in synthesizing multiple sources of evidence. One of the challenges too often confronted in synthesizing results is how to handle missing data. It stands to reason that the more we include multiple measures, methods, and sources in our data collection efforts, the more likely we are to have missing data. This is not to advocate for minimal data collection but to recognize the reality of many of our efforts. Strategies for dealing with missing data have been developed (see Little and Rubin, 1994, for example) and have implications for the working logic of evaluators.

Another challenge to synthesis, mentioned by House in Chapter Three as well as in earlier works (for example, House, 1994), is the absence of warrants with qualitative data. Fournier has defined a warrant as the way inferences drawn from evidence are supported and connected to the claim. As House indicates, there has not been the same amount of scrutiny and work on qualitative methods as there has been on quantitative methods. There are few controls on sources of bias, for example. In practice, therefore, it is difficult to derive claims or conclusions from qualitative data, particularly if they do not converge with quantitative data or if qualitative data are the only source of data in a study. Miles and Huberman (1994), as well as Yin (1994, 1993), have contributed a great deal to improving the rigor of the collection and analysis methods of these data. Rival hypothesis techniques can and should be applied in the analysis of qualitative data, but many of the methods and their application continue to require a great deal of judgment. As House mentions, this is an area still in need of additional work.

Presenting the Bottom Line. Getting to a bottom line is difficult, but communicating it is an equal challenge. Few of us are expert at framing our conclusions so that our mothers understand what we have found. Even when we can be clear in what we know, we often are not certain how strong to make the conclusions, particularly in the absence of a randomized design. Those trained in social science have few problems being cautious; in fact, if we are asked the implications of our data, we are often heard saying that we need additional research to obtain a better understanding of what we have. However, there may be times when we are overly cautious or, perhaps more aptly, too vague in our conclusions. There is a discomfort with a bottom line; multiple lines or conclusions feel more appropriate and comfortable. House acknowledges this discomfort and recognizes the need for multiple syntheses in certain situations while striving for the single synthesis. In House's view, collecting data from multiple stakeholders is important and "we should recognize the pluralism of society, but we also need—must have—ways of putting values and interests together again rationally" (House, p. xx).

Context does seem to play a role in the nature of the conclusions that can be communicated. Within the policy arena, the number of bottom lines presented diffuses the conclusions such that they are difficult to absorb. I am not advocating sound-bite conclusions or for the evaluator to be the philosopher-king, as mentioned by House, but rather for more attention to understanding the "message points" from a study and how to present them accurately and clearly. This is an area in which few of us receive training.

In a related vein, often we are in situations in which a decision is going to be made, with or without evaluation information. A decision is going to be made to renew or to discontinue a program. The question is this: can the evaluation we conduct inform the decision and reduce any of the uncertainty in the decision, even if the conclusions are not as definitive as we would like?

Here is another example from the trenches. As a relatively new evaluator to the legislative oversight arena, I was part of a team asked to evaluate a program that was coming up for renewal. The program was a diversion program for nonviolent offenders that had both fans and detractors in the legislature, as well as those who had not given it much attention. We were asked to evaluate whether the program was or was not reducing recidivism among participants and, in turn, whether it was reducing costs in the prison system. However, the follow-up period was deemed too short to conduct an adequate recidivism analysis. We did believe that we could address an important implementation question and at least indicate if the program was on the right track. That is, was it truly being used by judges as a diversion from incarceration or were there individuals being diverted to the program who otherwise might be placed on probation? If the program was doing the latter, then it would be unlikely that there would be cost savings. Probation was less costly than the program, whereas incarceration was vastly more costly.

We estimated how many individuals in the program would have otherwise been incarcerated with the use of a logic model following sentencing theory (Rog and Henry, 1987). We developed two estimates, one based on only individuals who could be classified by the model and another on all individuals in the sample. Our team felt that both estimates were important to consider; both yielded a sizable number being properly diverted, but there was a difference between the two estimates. However, the head of our agency felt that if we provided both estimates in the central part of the text (and the executive summary), we would not communicate the finding effectively. Therefore a decision was made to select the least controversial of the two estimates (both were less than what those in the correctional system believed was happening) and place the detailed explanation in the appendix. Thus a single explanation won out.

Providing Internal Explanations. In most evaluations, the answer to the primary question of program effectiveness is straightforward: it does not work. To be sure, often several caveats are called for—there may have been problems with the methodology, perhaps the measures were not sensitive enough or were not capturing all areas of potential outcome, and so on. These caveats are important but often do not fully explain why the program did not have an effect. The challenge for evaluators is to continue to make the results useful—to extend the role of the evaluation to determine not only what has worked or not but why that outcome has been obtained.

In our current evaluation of an initiative for homeless families, part of the intent of the program was to "create systems change" within nine cities funded. Given that the concept of *system* itself is not well defined, particularly when talking about a population that is so heterogeneous and spans across multiple systems, the evaluation was designed with a broad net of measures, methods, and sources. The theory developed by our client was minimalistic. There was little attention given to how change would occur, especially within the modest resources available, but there was more attention to what types of changes would be desirable.

The lack of detail in the theory underlying the systems component is common among the demonstration initiatives in operation that have systems change as a driving goal. The literature and the practice is quite lean with theory or expertise in how to bring about systems change. Therefore part of our reasoning, based on the problem and phenomena, was to build in rich descriptions of the systems that do exist and the system-building activity in the projects in addition to their accomplishment of systems change.

As we engaged in the evaluation, it became apparent that little systems change was being or would be accomplished in the projects. In an effort to provide more to the projects than documentation of the outcomes, and to show why systems change was not possible, we included an expanded explanation of systems in general. Our intent was to provide a more in-depth understanding of the phenomena—what are systems, what is the progression of activity that may lead to systems change, what are the intermediate sets of outcomes or substitute activities that occur, and what are the barriers to these outcomes and other outcomes. In essence, we developed an inventory of system activities to communicate what was happening in the projects and to provide a basis for further system-level study.

To Recommend or Not to Recommend. Scriven believes that evaluators often are not in a position to offer recommendations. He defines the evaluator's role more narrowly than others, often more narrowly than can be achieved in practice, but he does provide a set of boundaries and cautions around the role that are important to heed. Too often evaluators are thrust in positions to do more than their expertise and position allow. Evaluators typically are not in the position to develop a program or to scope out the next course of actions. However, that is not to say that the evaluators cannot assist the relevant parties in each of these areas through the practice of evaluation.

Patton (1994) suggests that evaluators can facilitate general recommendations by clients and users. Work groups and policy groups, such as those incorporated within evaluability assessment (for example, Wholey, 1979), offer a good vehicle for this facilitation. It provides an ongoing mechanism for others to understand the working logic of the evaluation and to develop recommendations with this logic in mind.

I do, however, agree with those in the field who believe evaluators should become more involved in the development and refinement of the programs that we evaluate. Reichardt (1994), for example, believes that it may be incumbent upon evaluators to develop the expertise that Scriven calls for in order to have a more active role in making recommendations for action. In addition, as Patton (1994) notes, although the facilitation of recommendations by others may be the best strategy in most evaluations, the gray-headed, experienced evaluator's ability to make recommendations should not be lightly disregarded.

Summary

The first four chapters in this volume offer both the theorist and the practitioner important, practical guidance in thinking about the reasoning process. In this chapter, I have highlighted those lessons and ideas from these chapters that resonate with my own experience. I also have attempted to offer some strategies for maintaining a clear reasoning process while reconciling day-to-day challenges. The issues that have presented challenges to me that have been discussed in this chapter include the nature of the role I am willing to play; fuzzy phenomena that are the focus of the evaluation; synthesizing vast amounts of data to reach a bottom line and then figuring out how to present this bottom line concisely; providing useful explanations when programs and policies do not work; and deciding when recommendations are within the evaluation role.

All evaluations, even those that have rigorous, carefully planned designs, still involve areas of judgment and decision. Rarely, however, has guidance been provided on how to make these judgments in a manner that is consonant with the reasoning process that drives the logic of the study. This chapter, together with this entire volume, aims to begin to fill the void in this area.

References

Edwards, P. "Conceptual and Methodological Issues in Evaluating Emergent Programs." *Evaluation and Program Planning*, 1987, *12*, 391–396.

Hedrick, T. E., Bickman, L., and Rog, D. J. *Applied Research Design*. Newbury Park, Calif.: Sage, 1993.

House, E. "The Future Perfect of Evaluation." *Evaluation Practice*, 1994, *15*, 239–248.

Little, R. A., and Rubin, D. B. *Statistical Analysis with Missing Data*. New York: Wiley, 1994.

Miles, M., and Huberman, A. M. *Qualitative Data Analysis*. Newbury Park, Calif.: Sage, 1994.

Patton, M. Q. "Developmental Evaluation." *Evaluation Practice*, 1994, *15*, 311–320.

Reichardt, C. S. "Summative Evaluation, Formative Evaluation, and Tactical Research." *Evaluation Practice*, 1994, *15*, 275–382.

Rog, D. J. "The Evaluation of the Homeless Families Program: Challenges in Implementing a Nine-City Evaluation." In D. J. Rog (ed.), *Evaluating Programs for the Homeless*. New Directions for Program Evaluation, no. 52. San Francisco: Jossey-Bass, 1991.

Rog, D. J. "Expanding the Boundaries of Evaluation: Strategies for Refining and Evaluating Ill-defined Interventions." In S. L. Friedman and H. C. Haywood (eds.), *Developmental Followup: Concepts, Genres, Domains, and Methods*. San Diego, Calif.: Academic Press, 1994.

Rog, D. J., and Henry, G. T. "An Implementation Evaluation of Community Corrections." *Evaluation Review*, 1987, *11*, 336–354.

Wholey, J. *Evaluation: Promise and Performance*. Washington, D.C.: Urban Institute, 1979.

Yin, R. *Applications of Case Study Research*. Newbury Park, Calif.: Sage, 1993.

Yin, R. *Case Study Research: Design and Methods*. Newbury Park, Calif.: Sage, 1994.

DEBRA J. ROG is research fellow at the Vanderbilt University Institute for Public Policy Studies, where she directs the Washington office of the Center for Mental Health Policy.

INDEX

Absolutism, 81
Acceptability, 74
Accessible, defined, 53
Activists, 55; bridging gap between, and purists, 60–61; logical problems with, 55–58
Alkin, M. C., 17, 54
American Evaluation Association (AEA), viii, 11
American Psychological Association (APA), 6
Amundson, R., 85
Applications level, 50
Argument, 72–73; in comparison to implication and inference, 72; schemes, 75–76
Arrow, K., 52
Arrow's impossibility theorem, 69
Ault, R. L., Jr., 6, 7, 8, 9

Backings, 24
Bickman, L., 94
Blair, J. A., 2, 3, 71, 74, 75, 76, 77, 79, 80
Bobo, L., 44
Bohannon, P., 86
Bottom-line, presentation of, 97–98
Bourbon, W. T., 86
Bradsher, K., 40
Brinkerhoff, R. O., 12
Bryk, A., 33

Campbell, D. T., 20, 25–26, 27
Causal approach, 84; explanation of, 20; illustrated, 21
Causal effectiveness, 27
Chamberlin, T. C., 12
Chircop, S., 12
Claims, 24; evaluative, 50
Coherence, 37; stages of deliberative process of, 37–38
Colorado, University of, 35; tenure requirement for, 35–36
Connoisseurial approach, 75, 84; explanation of, 20; illustrated, 21; working logic in, 83
Context, 87; and purpose, 83–84; House's view of, 84, 97
Cook, T. D., 18, 20, 22, 25–26, 27, 29, 33, 42, 44, 46
Credibility, 94

Criminal justice, 10
Criteria: acceptability, relevance, and sufficiency, 73–74; design trade-offs, for assessing, 94; line between indicators and, 65; of merit, 66: primary, 69: secondary, 69
Critical multiplism, 33
Cziko, G. A., 85

Darkes, J., 6
Data: methods for collecting, 41–42; missing, strategies for dealing with, 96
De jure versus de facto, 10
Decision alternatives, evaluation of, 62
Definitions: comparison of different, for same phenomenon, 23; concept of, in tradtional logic, 64
Dialectical, definition of, 76
Disclosure, 68
Diverse positions, accounting for differences between, 29–30

Educational Researcher, 85
Edwards, P., 95
Eisner, E. W., 12, 18, 20, 22
Ellett, F. S., 17
Equivocal death analysis (EDA), 6
Evaluand, defined, 68
Evaluate, defined, 16
Evaluatee, 68
Evaluation: bottom-line result of, 93, 96; in cognitive democracy, 44–47; defined, 51; distinguishing, from nonevaluation, 30; four distinctive basic operations of, 51; of fuzzy phenomena, 95–96; general logic of, 33, 73, 95: illustrated, 17, 20; informal logic and reasoning in, 71–80; inquiry strategies, 11–12; of *Iowa* explosion, 82; method, 50; parameters of, 11; practice, logic of, 49–70; practitioner and importance of reasoning, 93–99; societal games, 10–11; types, 50; working logic of, 94
Evaluation approaches. *See* Working logic
Evaluation theory, implications for practice and, 27–30
Evaluation Thesaurus, evaluation parameters in, 69

Ordering Information

NEW DIRECTIONS FOR EVALUATION is a series of paperback books that presents the latest techniques and procedures for conducting useful evaluation studies of all types of programs. Books in the series are published quarterly in Spring, Summer, Fall, and Winter and are available for purchase by subscription as well as by single copy.

SUBSCRIPTIONS for 1995 cost $56.00 for individuals (a savings of 22 percent over single-copy prices) and $78.00 for institutions, agencies, and libraries. Please do not send institutional checks for personal subscriptions. Standing orders are accepted. (For subscriptions outside of North America, add $7.00 for shipping via surface mail or $25.00 for air mail. Orders *must be prepaid* in U.S. dollars by check drawn on a U.S. bank or charged to VISA, MasterCard, or American Express.)

SINGLE COPIES cost $19.00 plus shipping (see below) when payment accompanies order. California, New Jersey, New York, and Washington, D.C., residents please include appropriate sales tax. Canadian residents add GST and any local taxes. Billed orders will be charged shipping and handling. No billed shipments to post office boxes. (Orders from outside North America *must be prepaid* in U.S. dollars by check drawn on a U.S. bank or charged to VISA, MasterCard, or American Express.)

SHIPPING (SINGLE COPIES ONLY): one issue, add $3.50; two issues, add $4.50; three issues, add $5.50; four to five issues, add $6.50; six to seven issues, add $7.50; eight or more issues, add $8.50.

DISCOUNTS FOR QUANTITY ORDERS are available. Please write to the address below for information.

ALL ORDERS must include either the name of an individual or an official purchase order number. Please submit your order as follows:
   Subscriptions: specify series and year subscription is to begin
   Single copies: include individual title code (such as PE59)

MAIL ALL ORDERS TO:
   Jossey-Bass Publishers
   350 Sansome Street
   San Francisco, California 94104-1342

FOR SUBSCRIPTION SALES OUTSIDE OF THE UNITED STATES, CONTACT:
   any international subscription agency or Jossey-Bass directly.

OTHER TITLES AVAILABLE IN THE
NEW DIRECTIONS FOR EVALUATION SERIES
Lois-ellin G. Datta, Editor-in-Chief